SELLING THE BIG TICKET

How to Manage the Multiple Approval Sale

BUCK BLESSING

RANDOM CHANCE PRESS
Rocky Hill, New Jersey

Copyright © 1994 by Buck Blessing
All rights reserved

RANDOM CHANCE PRESS
P.O. Box 379
Rocky Hill, New Jersey 08553-0379

Library of Congress Catalog Card Number: 94-74866

2nd Printing 1996

Designed and illustrated by Tracey O'Brien,

ISBN 0-9656474-0-4

Acknowledgements

I want to thank my clients, who have made this book, and much more in my life, possible; my wife Joan, whose editorial comments made every sentence better; and my salespeople, who initially used these ideas on faith alone.

Contents

Foreword
An Overview of the Concepts

1	The Way We Were	15
2	Showing Up	28
3	See Anybody Once	45
4	Pink Smoke	55
5	Selling the Goat	70
6	Getting to First Base	81
7	Marketing to Major Accounts	98
8	The Second Time Around – Act I	114
9	The Second Time Around – Act II	123
10	The Second Time Around – Act III	131
11	Magic Matters	142
12	Tools of the Trade	155
13	After the Sale	169
14	The World as a Work of Art	175

Foreword

Making a large sale is a most difficult, time-consuming task. But landing that big one can make a salesperson's year and, in a few cases, his or her career.

Many books have been written on how to analyze and develop tactics to win a major account. A few contain useful ideas for planning and managing your sales activities, but none deal directly with the only moments that really matter – those face-to-face interactions with the cast of characters that play a part in every major-account sale.

Selling the Big Ticket fills this gap. The best strategy and planning in the world never make a sale, they just get you to the prospect's front door. Every sale is made in a "close encounter" and every close encounter is what scientists call a "chaos" event, one in which you have some idea about what will happen, but the unexpected always occurs.

Selling the Big Ticket describes what you need to do to prepare for those critical face-to-face meetings. You will learn the only effective way to present yourself to the major account and the unique strategies you must use to make the big-ticket sale.

An Overview of the Concepts

The Issues Start

Selling The Big Ticket features a different opening to the selling process than the current consultative approach. I believe you need to put value on the table early. Your prospect wants a quick answer to the question: "Why should I listen, answer questions or spend time with you?"

An "issues start" presents, with precision and insight, the organizational issues your product most effectively solves. You must give prospects a reason early to listen, to connect with you, to stay awake, to move you to the next step.

That early reason is what I call value. Value can be your brilliant mind, the energy you radiate, your good looks. Who knows? Not all of us can deliver on those attributes but we all can deliver value through the issues start.

Managing the Multiple-Approval Sale

Much sales training focuses on the closing presentation. I believe that meeting is often a ritual formality. Today you have a tougher job. Businesses are like fortresses. Security checks, gatekeepers, voice mail make it difficult if not impossible to connect with your prospect. While the impact of teambuilding and powersharing strategies has made the work place more fair and open, it has diffused power so thoroughly that rarely is one person ever responsible for a decision. The smallest step forward requires multiple approvals.

Today you're lucky if you talk to the same person twice. The boss changes, the company's been bought, merged, reorganized or bankrupted. The problem needed to be solved yesterday, yet a call today may bring the information that it no longer matters. Problems can exist and nobody knows, or more likely, nobody cares – and for sure nobody is responsible.

Marketing is the Key to Success

It is said that marketing techniques extend from product research to within three feet of the buyer. Apparently, from 36 inches in, it should be all sales pitch (closing techniques, overcoming objections, etc.). In effect, marketing ends and selling begins in that face-to-face encounter between buyer and seller. I don't agree. You must use marketing techniques – positioning, differentiation, niche-building – throughout the process. Positioning your product relative to the competition creates prospect interest. It helps the buyer differentiate between competing products. Talking differences, rather than selling product features, establishes you as unique.

While a great deal of competition may exist against your wares, there can be none against differences.

Further, traditional selling approaches, whether emphasizing product features, advantages and benefits or the more recent consultative techniques, have the potential, if not used carefully, to antagonize one or more of the multiple approvers of a big-ticket purchase. For example, a product push can easily be perceived as insensitive. On the other hand, sharp questioning early in the selling process can backfire, especially when an approver doesn't have the answers. Marketing, rather than selling your products, is a safer strategy for those initial encounters leading to the sale.

Creating the Energy for Action

All too often, the statements we make to a buyer fail to state our case as powerfully as possible. We use cold, logical language – "Our service for XYZ resulted in a profit increase of …"– when emotion, even passion, is needed to get the process moving. Well-crafted, succinct stories create energy for action. Stories are educational, real. People learn by analogy. If, in addition, the story hits the mark, good! If not, the story suggests questions, observations, e.g., "Why did they do it that way? Our problem is not like that."

Stories sell. A story can turn an "issue" into "trouble" for a prospect. They begin to see that the future will be darker if they don't take action. People pay money to get rid of trouble. Getting rid of an issue is less pressing. Very few prospects have a good sense or understanding of their issue. As long as it remains vague, a little out of focus, mañana is good enough. Clear sharp, anecdotes describing how this issue, if unaddressed, can become serious, help the seller move the prospect to action.

Often, stories are simply "weather reports" that have little effect on making the sale. *Selling The Big Ticket* shows you how to build stories that generate energy and commitment. You will own what you talk about. That's the difference between a story that generates excitement and a dull dreary tale that sucks the life out of a room.

Building Alliances

Every sales approach says relationships matter, but most of them offer little counsel beyond that. The topic is often avoided because of the difficulty in describing a good relationship, or how to form one, without having the prose turn into woo-woo. The advice seems better suited to making friends than making sales. Yet, building a good relationship with your customers is your most important job.

In today's volatile, complicated business environment, delivery is becoming ever the more important part of the purchase. Before the sale, delivery is only your promises. You may have a "money-back guarantee." Your specs may be equal to or better than the competitors'. But as Mark Twain has observed, there are "lies, damned lies and statistics." How does a customer make a decision in the face of these "statistics" and in an increasingly competitive world with less and less product differentiation and more and more "knock-off" products? Client belief in your promises depends solely on the quality of your relationship with them.

Showing Up

Some sales approaches suggest you mimic the style and behavior of the client or prospect. Others recommend a specific role or manner you need to effect. Usually, this advice comes equipped with enough fancy and obscure language to qualify as rocket science. I don't believe it works. Today's sales cycles are so long that any dissonance or incongruity between what you are and what you pretend to be will be picked up by the client. A little pretense is usually enough to bring the sale to a dead stop. No sales stars will shine for long if they lose customer trust. Showing up – projecting your unique, memorable self – is critically important in selling the major account.

How the World Works

If you want to be a really top performer, not simply another journeyman, you must know how the world works. I believe salespeople and, for that matter, most people have been seriously misled. Sales gurus, behavioral scientists, management theorists describe a world that functions in predictable ways. People are sensible and do sensible things. It's a rational world. No UFOs, magic or moods. Frankly, I've never seen that world. The one I live and sell in is crazy. People buy for any damn reason or for none at all. Moods make people. There's magic in every sale. You can't go by the book and make it big. You have to improvise, create, be an artist, be a star. *Selling The Big Ticket* will help you to expect the unexpected, to hope for it because it's where the opportunity lies. You already know the world is wacky. You are not alone. You will find some new ways to make this non-rational, random, serendipity-filled world work for you.

Chapter 1
The Way We Were

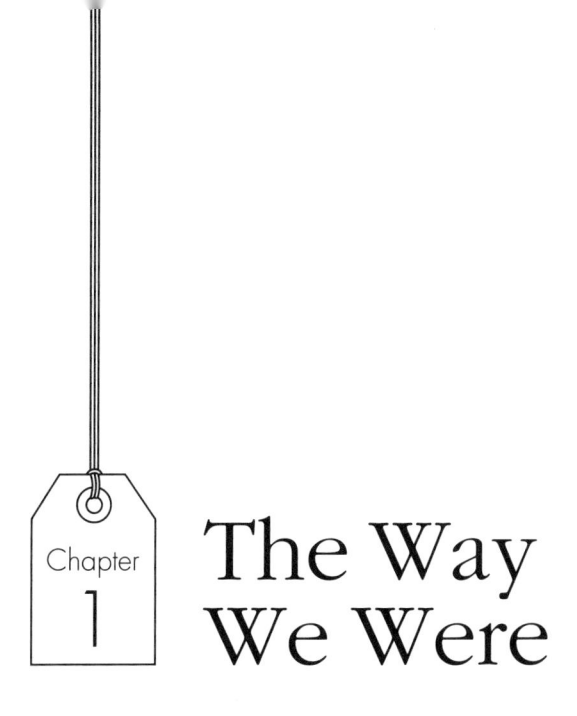

"That old man river just keeps rollin', he just keeps rollin' along." Those lyrics from the musical *Show Boat* describe U.S. businesses in the middle of the 20th century about as well as any scientific treatise. Change was gradual and slow. Competition generally meant shared markets. In any event, there was enough business to go around. Predicting the future seemed easy. Five-year plans, ten-year plans were written on vellum, bound and distributed to all executives. The emphasis was on process and method. Forecasting made a lot of sense when you pretty well knew what was around the next bend. Salespeople were trained to sell on a vast commercial Mississippi – wide, deep, slow-moving.

In the last ten years, our Mississippi has turned into a Colorado River, filled with rapids of unanticipated change, increasing complexity and confusion. The organizations we belong to and those we sell to are caught up in the white waters of fierce competition, reorganization and shifting priorities. It seems every business is asking: Who are we? Where are we going? Where should we be going? How will we get there? No good answers seem to have emerged. Just about the time some vision or strategy is in place, our world fractures or metastasizes into something else. Economic forests become deserts overnight. Oceans of revenue dry up.

Complexity

We face complexity everywhere we turn – in the cars we drive and can no longer repair ourselves; in the modern office with its FAX, computers, intricate phone systems only the most diligent can master; in our homes stuffed with more advanced electronics than the equipment that took us to the moon.

Desktop computers can handle ten million instructions per second. It took over 900 people to program the combat computer for the Navy's Seawolf submarine. In 1992, three faulty bits of code, in 2.1 million lines of instructions in a single switching gear from one of 15 suppliers, knocked out telephone service in Washington D.C., Los Angeles, Pittsburgh and the Northeast corridor for over twelve hours. Complexity didn't gradually creep up on us. It dropped like a bomb.

Touch-tone phones arrived in 1965. Not only were they quicker to use than the rotary dial, they changed the way we communicate with each other. Voice-mail, FAX technology, the ability to ring New Zealand directly, were only a few results. A query to United Air Lines for frequent-flyer information can be handled without ever talking to a living human being. Last year some Ohio residents were able to file their income tax return – 1040EZ – through their touch-tone phones. Touch-tones not only made the world work faster, they made a part of it into something brand new and different.

The complexity of modern life is completely changing how we sell. Just a few years ago (it only *seems* like light years), you identified your buyer (singular) by title (perhaps Purchasing Agent) and made contact. With a little luck, you would eventually connect.

With mergers, acquisitions, strange organizational theories put into practice by hopeful CEOs, your buyer has become invisible. Finding out who needs your "stuff" in a large organization can be almost impossible. You don't know a title, and your queries to receptionists are met with frosty replies usually reserved for ex-husbands late on the alimony. Finally you think you might be on to someone. However, they're never in. All you get is that somewhat disconnected speech on the voice mail saying that they're "not here right now but will return your call soon." Which they don't.

In addition, your product is usually complex enough (a drip coffee maker or postage machine will do) to require more than one approval. Finding all the buyers takes time and about the point everything is in place, the priorities are changed.

Competition

Competition has changed the selling job, too. The idea that competition has always been around has been around for so long that a lot of people believe it's true. It isn't! *Real* choice or competition only became a fact in the early '60s.

It was only after Europe and Asia had rebuilt their industrial base, after World War II, that true competition became an unpleasant reality.

Prior to 1960, many markets were shared. Ford, Chrysler and GM made a lot of racket about competing, but it was all much ado about a few percentage points of market share. Customers were "hyped" but never really consulted about their needs. Costs were simply passed along to the consumer. And the automobile companies weren't unique. Banks and grocery stores, for example, had greater demand than they could, or in some cases wanted to, meet. The only restraint on meeting the demand was the ability or desire to open new branches or add more people.

In addition, the U.S. was still predominantly made up of small towns that were geographically close, but distant in communications. There was little awareness of what others were doing or buying. In 1950, 10% of the population had a TV. By 1960, 85% had one and access to all the information that came through it. In 1957, there were no commercial jet planes, no FAX machines, and only a few Xerox machines. The sales job was mostly about convincing the prospect to buy "one," i.e., whatever you were selling. Customer awareness of alternatives was low and choices were few.

The foreign invasion of commercial and personal products along with improved communications made true competition a reality. Now salespeople had to sell "against" other products. Buyers wanted to know just how a product was different from another. Salespeople not only had to know their own product but others as well. Overnight, you had to be a lot smarter to be a good salesperson. Talking "differences" is a higher-level mental exercise than talking "features and benefits." You had to learn a lot more about your customers so you could talk about a difference that made a difference to them.

Competition changed the sales job in other ways. Competitors not only brought products to the market, but also tons of information – evaluations, studies, tests, testimonials – all of which showed their products in the most favorable light. Competition brought choice all right, but it also brought confusion for buyers. The 1994 Video Review buyer's guide details 352 TV models, 240 video recorders, 148 camcorders, and more to come. It's mind-boggling! A degree in electrical engineering might help, but not much.

Consciousness

A lot more than the products we sell and the competition we face has changed. People have different *expectations* about products and services. As a young man in the '50s, I searched for the restaurant that really "put on a spread." Give me food, lots of it. Today, young and old alike look for freshness, quality, attractive presentation, etc. We've moved away from greater quantity to higher *quality*. Quantity can be measured, quality is a more elusive concept. In addition to good taste, it's a vision, an image, an excitement, an energy. You must be able to create these kinds of intangible differences to successfully sell your products and services.

Individual awareness has taken a quantum leap in the last couple of generations. There is as much information in one issue of the *New York Times* as the average person in Europe was exposed to in a lifetime during the 16th century. In 1960, 160 women received MBAs in the United States. In 1991, 221 received MBAs from Harvard alone. In 1950, only one person in five had any college experience and only one person in ten had a degree. By 1980, 50% had been to college and 25% had degrees. We might argue about how good this education really is, but we can't deny that people are learning a lot more about the world around them and how it works. These new buyers know how to compare and question.

By the time they are 18 years old, kids have watched an average of 24,000 hours of television. They've seen every ploy, every kind of subtle con, dozens of times. They know when they're being manipulated, even at the hands of a skilled practitioner, and they resent it. These are today's prospects and clients. They are not provincial bumpkins or clucks to be swindled into seeing the two-headed lady at the county fair. One hundred surefire closes just might be one hundred ways to lose a sale.

Confusion

Sorting out the players in a multiple-approval sale is like trying to pin down "Who's on First?" in the old Abbott and Costello routine. In the long ago and far away, you sold to hierarchical organizations that looked like this:

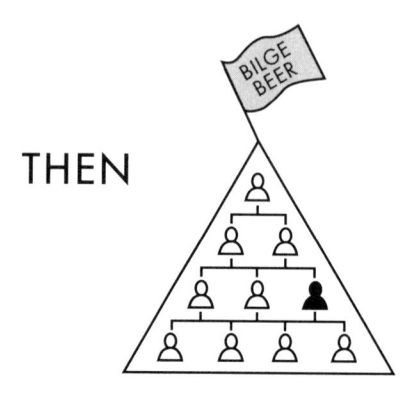

THEN

Typically you called on a guy – late thirties, mid-forties. This was either the only company he had worked for or his second. He planned to retire from this outfit. He occupied a known niche at Bilge Beer. Today that organization looks more like this:

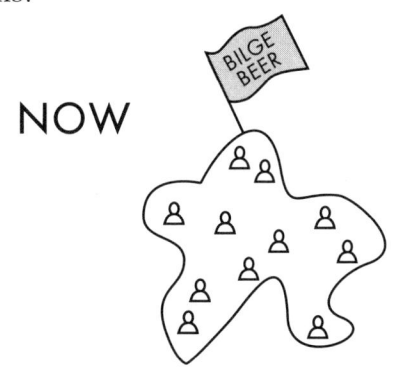

... and your guy is nowhere to be found. Or once discovered, he soon vanishes.

When you do find a real buyer, you can be sure he or she needs a "special" version of your product or service. So now you have to make two sales. You sold Bilge Beer, now you need to sell your organization on delivering the custom package. This is often your toughest sale.

Remember, your organization is not immune to our changing universe. It too has become a fuzzball.

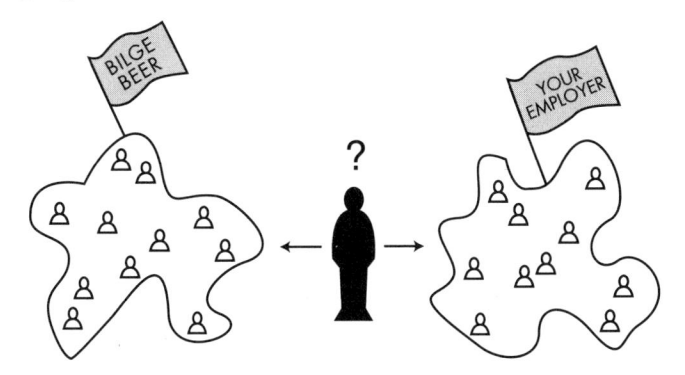

So you have to organize the team, persuade others not under your control to help, and convince "the powers that be" to go along. According to sales trainers at one General Electric division, 70% of their salespeople's time is spent selling internally.

Thirty years ago we sold on a placid river. The scenery slowly drifted by. Today it's all white water. Shooting a Level 3 rapid requires very different skills and, more importantly, different beliefs on what it takes to succeed, than guiding a stern-wheeler down the Mississippi. Today's reality is too complex and uncertain for the traditional sales techniques. It's not that the old rules can't work anymore, but rather that they simply are insufficient to do the job.

David Osborne, co-author of *Reinventing Government*, describes the challenge to organizations in this way: "To be effective in these times, institutions (public or private) must be flexible, adaptable and innovative. They must search constantly for new ways to improve services and heighten productivity." How many times have you read or heard similar comments about the organizations we sell to? And, no doubt about it, organizations are moving in this direction. You must be at least as assertive, creative and flexible to successfully sell these new organizations.

Out of the Dark Ages

I've been selling services since 1966. Early on, I sold management training. Then in late 1972, I joined with Tod White to form Blessing/White, Inc. We had an idea; we would design a workshop to help individuals take more personal responsibility for their on-the-job performance. In effect, learn to self-manage.

Sounds pretty tame in the '90s, but 20 years ago it was considered radical, maybe even Communistic, by more than a few business people. The early '70s were the apogee for the traditional command and control organization. The big boys (it was all boys then) would make decisions on the top floors of the Bilge Beer Building and then let them seep down through layers of management to the rank and file at the bottom.

In some companies, management was just a euphemism for petty tyrants and blustering bureaucrats. Initiatives from below were often stifled with "Hey, we're not paying you to think." I know. That comment was directed to me more than once, during the nine years I spent as a tool and diemaker in the automobile industry, prior to getting into sales. I thought that was a dumb way to run a business and the decline of our domestic auto industry has furnished the proof of its bankruptcy.

Tod and I had another wild idea. We would sell this workshop – Managing Personal Growth (MPG) – not to individuals, but to their employers. We believed businesses would pay to see their employees become more autonomous and productive. As you might imagine, the first few years were pretty lean. I remember calling on the Director of Training and Development at the ITT Corporation in 1973. As I told my story, his face took on a look of quiet amazement and incredulity. After my spiel, he said no, he didn't think ITT needed any of my stuff, and as we walked to his office door, he put his hand on my shoulder and said gently, "Lots of luck, fella."

In those early years, we did manage to find a few companies who shared our philosophy – Michigan Bell, Univac, Parke-Davis, Kinney Shoes, et al. And we also learned a lot about selling a product without a sharp edge or focus (MPG was about as tangible as Unitarianism) to large organizations.

A "soft" product like MPG could never be purchased by one person on his or her own. There were always several people who had to say yes. Some we knew about from our initial contacts within the organization. Other approvers and "wannabe" approvers would show up during the sales cycle. Then there were other folks who didn't need to say yes, but could say no and kill the deal. We, to our dismay, usually only found these people after they said that bad word.

As more people got into the act, the sales cycle grew longer and longer. A big deal could easily take a year or more to put together or fall apart. Often, when you have everything in place, a key player would get promoted, fired, or just lose interest in the project.

Invariably, there was some chance encounter, some "accident" or serendipity that would bring the deal together or open the door to another selling opportunity. The organizational world didn't seem to work the way the business texts said it did, i.e., in a cool, rational, ordered manner.

Most of the selling ideas I had learned were not much help. They had lots of advice on how to sell one person one clean, specific well-defined product or service. The sales books were filled with aphorisms like "close early and close often." Wow, that sounded great. Unfortunately, closing on people who needed to approve, but couldn't authorize the purchase, made them look impotent and usually got the door closed in my face. Those ideas might work for a small-ticket, low-consequence purchase, but for the big deal, multiple-approval, customized sale, forget it.

Yet, even today, books filled with this useless advice clutter the book racks at all our airports. Is there anybody out there still selling a simple off-the-shelf product to one buyer? I doubt it.

Every customer wants a custom job. And with the advent of teambuilding and powersharing, no one person says yes on his or her own about anything, including the weather.

In the '70s, consultative sales techniques came on the scene. Overnight, salespeople became more professional (only natural fibers would touch their bodies) and scientific. Salespeople became business needs consultants, problem solvers. The sale became a mathematical cost-benefit transaction. This approach sounded and looked great, but my world never seemed to unfold according to the plan. The diagnostic questions were fine, but finding somebody with the answers was the hard part. Very rarely did I meet a real buyer on the first or even the second call. I needed a guide to the maze as much as I needed a buyer.

As Blessing/White became more successful (by 1990 we had over 300 clients and more than one million people had attended an MPG seminar), we began to hire the best salespeople we could find. Most came to us with strong sales skills and a proven record of success. Several came from companies that sold sales training seminars. These folks had had more than a little sales training! Yet it would take them over a year to get up to speed.

Clearly, MPG was a different kind of product than they had sold previously. In many ways, it was typical of today's products and services: It could be used to solve more than one problem; different parts of an organization could buy and therefore wanted a say in the purchase; it could be adapted or modified for a client.

These are the characteristics of today's major-account sale. The seller talks about the capabilities of his or her organization and modifies the product package to meet the buyer's specifications. But because the product becomes a bit fuzzy during this process, more and more people in the buyer's organization sense that this transaction might, could, should affect them. The political games come into play. Calculations are made about who will win, lose or cause someone else to lose face in the transaction. Who's responsible for what becomes vague and uncertain. A lassitude comes over the sales cycle.

Although the consultative approach was an improvement over the close early, close often school, it became very clear to me that sales skills *and* political skills were needed to close a major account. Making a multiple-approval sale required a knowledge of basic techniques for sure, but technique alone never made the sale. You had to have a "feel," a kind of sixth sense about what was going on and what to do next.

As the years went by, I developed my own ideas on selling the major account and began training my salespeople in them. I deeply believe that how you as a seller present yourself to the world, and what you believe about the world, is as important for sales success as what you do in a specific sales situation. The business world has changed so much that current sales techniques are incomplete and, in some cases, counterproductive to sales success.

An organization is like a beehive. A bee swarm has a kind of collective brain and personality. Some swarms are friendly and open. Others, downright hostile. Organizations are the same. They have personalities, moods, volatility. A change in the corporate climate can affect a large organization as much as the weather can affect a beehive.

Learning how to sell one bee is useless, you have to know how to affect the collective consciousness of the organization. You have to educate the client, trust your intuition (rational analysis can't cut through the incomprehensible complexity of a major sale) and believe in magic to make it big. Selling the major account is truly as much art as science.

My interest in the problems salespeople must handle in this changing, increasingly complex world continues to grow. Today's salespeople are truly on the cutting edge. You must design the product, provide leadership, sell the client and then persuade your employer to deliver the deal. It's a big job and it requires much bigger ideas than simply improved selling techniques.

Chapter 2 Showing Up

The initial response to greater complexity in corporate life was to fight with more complexity. Computer against computer. Byzantine organization structures like matrix management were designed to meet this challenge. Sales theorists responded much the same way. The contemporary literature is filled with enough complicated terminology to warm any scientist's heart.

There are positive deviations, polarity responders, negative imbedded commands, implication questions, explicit needs, implicit needs, response modes, relationship tension indicators, style markers and more. Rocket science at its best.

There are seven rules, twelve steps, fifteen techniques, specific procedures, questionnaires, diagnostic worksheets. Just follow the yellow brick road to sales fame and fortune.

Clearly, the best of these books have a lot to offer. Sales, like any profession, requires a knowledge of basic technique.

But technique alone will not make you a star. Take professional golf, for example. There are literally thousands of young aspiring golfers with excellent technique, yet only a handful will make it to the Tour. Why? What is it that separates those few from the rest?

It is certainly not more technique. Yet some will pursue the illusion that improved mechanics will make the difference. As any Saturday golfer knows, the toughest six inches in the game is between the ears. What turns a golfer into a star is not just technique, but a "feel" for the game.

The same is true for selling the big ticket. We all know salespeople who have the drill down pat, yet fail to get results. They are "over-mechanized," usually extremely logical, but they lack the touch that it takes to succeed. They are hackers to the end.

Selling the major account, like golf, is a game of both mechanics and feel. That *feel* is the art of a profession. It starts where the technique ends. Star salespeople always have that feel for the game; a seemingly effortless charm and grace at the point of attack with the client. They appear larger than life with their shrewd insights and creative solutions. They bring to their work a unique sensitivity, a rhythm, an intuitive sense of what the next correct step should be.

Anyone hoping to achieve success selling major accounts must bring these magical qualities to the face-to-face encounters with the client. You need more than procedures or logic to cut through the complexity surrounding the transaction. No scientific analysis will help you understand the tangled web of relationships and politics you need to sort out. No mechanical routines will save the day. As the chess grand master, Roman Dzindzichashvili said after an improbable victory, "I had to do a little magic to win."

We all have experienced the sales calls where we knew we could handle anything coming our way. We were in control. We were relaxed and confident. We had a certain panache. Defining this quality is impossible, but we know when we're "in the zone," as athletes call their transcendent performances, or when we see it in someone else. Stars in every field simply have more of these moments than others.

Star Quality

But do you really want to be a star? Taking a high profile seems risky. The Japanese have an expression, "deru kugiwa utareru" (the nail that protrudes will be hammered down), that seems apt. People are ever hopeful that some mechanism, procedure, bureaucracy, MBA degree will keep them warm and safe.

Perhaps such a haven exists, but not for salespeople. You are the proponent of change. You're selling risk (there is always some risk in any purchase). A "hunker down" sales personality is likely to communicate the very message you're working to diffuse. If you're always "playing it safe" don't expect any customer to "go for the gold."

Customers look for leadership as the world grows more complex and its problems appear less solvable. There's a huge hunger to connect with a real human being. Many people sense they're riding a bus without a driver. Clearly, you can't bring more uncertainty into this existential fog. In these turbulent times, you must take charge. Being out front requires some courage. As a major-account seller aspiring to stardom, you are trying to stay on the front edge of the wave, not in it. You need to be a star!

Becoming a star in sales, as in all of life, starts inside out, not outside in. It requires no special genius. There's no need to concoct some dramatic persona, buy a 6-oz. gold Rolex, or take up bungee-jumping. It does require that you be special and, luckily, you already are. All you need is the courage to be yourself. Just show up – warts and all.

Astronomers see all kinds: supernova, quasars, black holes, white dwarfs. A star is never well-rounded, evenly balanced, smoothly contoured. Each one is an unpredictable, spectacular phenomenon. So ... no roles, no modelling, no posturing, no mimicking of styles. Just downright irregular, unique, lopsided you. In other words, a star. No one can be sure how you'll show up, but you will be seen as somebody special.

I've been to a lot of meetings where nobody showed up. Oh, there were bodies in the room, but they all arrived in masks and costumes – playing out the role as Vice President of Engineering, or Marketing Consultant, or somebody's subordinate. No real people were there, only actors. It was as if they got up in the morning and put a tape in their internal VCR and just "let her rip." We're all concerned that we might look foolish, might make a mistake, might hurt our careers by doing what comes naturally, so we think of work as a stage play where we act out our part and hope to get a leading role eventually. But nobody has a relationship with a videotape (unless they're really strange). Relationships only exist between two live flesh and blood people.

If you show up, you just might get your customers to show you a glimpse of themselves. Two "masked men" can't form much more than a gruesome twosome. And if you plan to make a sale, you better find out who they really are and what they want, really want from the relationship. Showing up is not as dangerous as you might think; being a bit vulnerable just might make you a bit more loveable.

Most sales-training experts would agree that you are unlikely to make a major multiple-approval sale without an internal supporter, a champion. Most offer advice on finding one. But that's not the way it works. A champion finds you. He or she will join or start your fan club. How does that happen? By you showing up.

Showing up is easier than attempting to mirror the other person's behavior – the monkey see, monkey do sales approach. And playing a role is a lot like doing a paint-by-numbers picture. No matter how well it's done, you both wind up in the basement. Showing up as yourself is better than trying to live by artificial rules.

Are you scared that your weaknesses will be all too apparent? Just think about this for a moment. If you are absolutely certain the warts will show, isn't the opposite also true? – that your strengths will be visible as well? Give people a chance to admire you, a reason to do business with you. Let them see your strengths. Bring your real self to work every day. Show up!!

Make Mistakes

Once you show up, you'll make mistakes. That's O.K. Only through failure do you learn how good you really are. A tennis player with a "hot" serve who never faults in a match will never know just how well she can play. She has to hit a few long or short with power before she can say, "That's the edge."

Lots of folks claim to be risk-takers, but somehow they never have a failure. Risk is making mistakes, errors. Errors of commission. Top salespeople make lots of mistakes. Losers never make one. Just ask them.

When I first started in the training business, I had a great chance for a big sale to a major TV network. I thought they might well buy a thousand sets of training materials. When I got to the decisive meeting, the network president was in attendance. I could feel that everything was right for a big buy. But it didn't happen. They ordered one hundred sets and the program dribbled along and died.

Are you wondering why that big sale was lost? It was pretty simple: I never asked! You see, my business was just getting started and fifty sets was a big order. Like all start-ups, we needed every order, so I played it real safe just like the timid tennis player. Oh, I got an order, but I could have been a star.

I learned my lesson, though. Later on, when I was managing my own salespeople, I always told them, "Look, before you're going to be any good, you must make at least ten big blunders. Get started." Sophocles in 450 B.C. said it more eloquently: "You must learn by doing the thing, for though you think you know it, you can have no certainty until you try."

Mistakes make you learn in a hurry because they cause pain. They get your attention. Don't spend energy trying to cover them up; figure out how to do better. Ask yourself:

- Why did I lose the sale?
- Where did I go wrong?
- At what point did I lose the prospect?
- Was the cause what I *did* or how I *showed up*?
- What will I do differently the next time?

Making it big in service and system sales demands that you risk walking the high wire. Mediocre salespeople spend a lot of time learning to stay on it; the star has to know how to fall off and survive.

Few ideas look good the first time out. If you say, "I'll wait until I've thought through my idea completely before I present it," it will never get better. Ideas improve by trying them in the marketplace of your colleagues. They might say, "Oh, don't be crazy." So what? A really creative idea almost always looks crazy in the beginning.

In 1801, William Hazlitt, the English essayist, asked the richest man in London, "Sir, to what do you attribute your success?" The man replied, "Three words – impudence, impudence, impudence." So, if you're in a hurry to make it in this life, take a few chances. As the saying goes, it's easier to get forgiveness than permission.

Build on Strengths

Build on your strengths. It seems a simple bit of advice. Yet how many of us use the limited time we have for training to build on a known strength? Most of us choose or are advised by our boss to work on our weaknesses. And we do! Yet it's mighty hard to turn a weakness into a strength. About the most we can expect is competence.

If you work only on your weaknesses, one day you'll be a perfectly mediocre human being. Think about it. You focus on your weaknesses. Eventually they reach the O.K. level, but meanwhile, your talents atrophy. You've become an all-around person. All-around people are all around. That may be good enough for some, but it's not good enough to build the strong relationships with your clients that you need for sales success in the 1990s.

Real stars in the world we live in already know this message. Take Reggie Jackson. He was a great hitter, but unfortunately, a poor fielder. Yet I can tell you that every day when Reggie Jackson took practice, he practiced hitting the ball. He got to baseball's Hall of Fame by hitting home runs. He knew what he needed to do to be a star!

I have a top-performing saleswoman. A great closer, as they say, but lousy about submitting her expense reports. What should I do? In the old world we would train that saleswoman to file an accurate, timely expense report. In the classic command and control system, if she didn't get better, I, as her manager, would punish her. That is a sure route to failure in this new world. She can close deals, so I'll send her to school to learn how to do that even better. And I'll find somebody to do her expense reports for her. That's the difference. Just think about it. In an orchestra, you don't teach a great flute-player how to play the violin simply because he or she doesn't know how.

Learn to do better what you do best. Focus on what makes you valuable to your organization and your customers. Ask yourself:

- How am I unique, special, different from my peers, other salespeople?
- What are my strengths?
- How can I do more of what I do best?
- How can I do better what I do best?

Be a "Four-Thirds" Professional

He was a perky young man – tasseled, spit-shined Guccis, inky black pinstripes, a freshly baked MBA – who knew all about interfacing, empowering, visioning, being consultative. No doubt about it, he was lighter than air. He would need lead weights in those loafers to keep him grounded.

If it looks like a duck, acts like a duck and quacks like one, it must be a duck. That's common sense at work and at its worst. There are lots of folks who look, act and talk like professionals, but they're not. They're what I call "two-thirds." They're loaded with sales process and personality – the low-key, feel-good persona currently in style.

The young professional of my story followed the "program" to the letter. Lots of calls, follow-up letters out in less than three days. Four months later, he was searching for answers. "They (the prospects) seem to be asking for more" was his comment to his manager. After a brief discussion, it was obvious he had not studied any product information nor looked closely at his own product or those of the competition. He had had a half day of product familiarization and felt that was "good enough." He thought his job was to push a shopping cart for customers and ask what they wanted in it! He was "two-thirds" and it wasn't all his fault.

A true professional is "four-thirds." What puts you over the top are product knowledge and pride in your job.

For years salespeople have been overmechanized, taught that process was all you needed. Somebody forgot to tell them they needed to *know* something as well. A professional can't know too much about his product or service. Today's customers expect technical expertise from you on your product and your competition as well. If you don't know, who does? Certainly not your prospect. She has her hands full coping with the ever-changing, convoluted product or service she delivers to *her* clients.

Salespeople can fail for a lot of reasons, but in my personal experience, the majority of failures were product knowledge weaknesses. They didn't know how their product worked, how it could be modified (nobody wants anything off the shelf), what problems it solved, how it was different from the competition, or, more fundamentally, why their company was in business at all – other than to make money. Ultimately, it's your belief in your product that sells, and the only way to get that belief is to understand the product to the marrow of your bones. Use it! Deliver it! Maintain it! Handle customer complaints. Compare it to the competition. Write about it. Learn its strengths, its weaknesses. Talk to users. Be able to answer these questions perfectly:

- Why is my company in business at all?
- How are we different and better than our competition?
- What results does our service deliver? *Why do we do it the way we do?*
- What is our mission? What is our view of how the world works?
- What are the weaknesses of our product or service?
- What problems does our product solve? Why?
- How does our system work? *Why was it designed that way?*
- What are some great success stories?

If you've never answered those questions, do it now. Do it with some colleagues. You will all be more effective and more attractive at every call you make. And if you're an experienced professional, answer them again. You're going to get some different answers.

Don't dismiss this point about product knowledge. Remember, everything – including your products and your organization – is in white water these days. Building a sturdy raft of product knowledge will help you survive the turbulence.

Willy Loman, in Arthur Miller's *Death of a Salesman,* discovered that a smile and a shine can't carry the day. However, some poor salesfolks still believe it can. My mother decided to build a new home. This would be her best (and last) chance to achieve "the perfect house." To that end, she and Dad attended every open house in Kalamazoo to gather ideas. She got a few ideas, but she got more than a little angry. It seems most of the salespeople couldn't answer the simplest questions about the property they were showing: "Where are the lot lines?"; "What school district is this place in?"; "What are the taxes?"; "What kind of roof?" Their responses ranged from "I don't know" to "I'm not sure" to "It's probably in the paper work." Their ineptitude was too much for Mom, who had been a pretty fair saleswoman in her day. No more open houses for her (to Dad's relief).

Every topnotch salesperson I've known had total and absolute belief in their product. These were ordinary people who turned themselves into stars because they studied their product. They knew it inside out. The only way you can deliver a custom job to a customer is through your technical expertise. You'll be counted out if you're counting on someone else to do this job for you.

The "fourth third" is pride. Twenty years ago I lost faith in the product I was selling. It was a terrific job and I didn't want to leave. I agonized. Three little kids to support can keep you in line. I temporized. After a year, I quit. Not much of a story, but it had one surprising twist – all my customers later told me that they knew I had lost the faith. Yet, believe me, during that year I had been more evangelical than ever.

Obviously, confidence in your product contributes to pride in your work, but you must also be proud of your company and your colleagues. If you don't believe in your product or question the competency or ethics of your organization, start looking elsewhere. It's amazing how transparent our feelings are to our customers. Be proud or be gone.

Take responsibility for your ideas and actions. Everybody uses this "we" language. If something goes wrong close to home, "We screwed up" is the answer. If the screw-up is back at the office, "They screwed up."

Forget "we." Bring "I" back into your life and language. If you screw up, admit it. If your company screwed up, fix it. Remember, "We ought to do something" translates into either you do it or it won't get done.

Don't be like former D.C. Mayor Marion Barry who, convicted of cocaine possession, stood tall by proclaiming, "This human being stands here ready to say I'm sorry for the poor judgments that have happened to me." Or like William Aramony, ex-president of United Way of America, who, being forced to resign after egregious high-living on the corporate expense account, apologized for "lack of sensitivity to perception." Or like the driver of the pick-up truck that late one evening came crashing into my neighbor's living room. This woozy, bleary-eyed, quite drunk fellow climbed down from the cab, stared at my neighbor and exclaimed, "You're lucky I wasn't killed!"

Be proud enough to stand up and be counted. That's the start of courage and leadership.

Being a sales professional is more than clean business suits. It's your carriage and demeanor. It means understanding your responsibilities:

- You are an expert on your clients and the needs your product solves.

- You are an expert on your company and your product.

- You are in charge of the selling process.

If you want to make it big in this increasingly complex world, go four-thirds of the way. Two-thirds folks never get to the finish line.

Be Willing to Improvise

Your stardom depends on your ability to improvise. No two sales situations are the same; no one sales situation remains the same. Some sales managers push for scripts. Not content with being dull themselves, they wish to cause it in others.

Forget scripts! You cannot mold the future from the past. Start out with a loose plan, but if success or failure get in its way, alter it. Responding to the situation in front of you is the essential step from monologue to dialogue. Somebody out there will know you're reacting to their needs, appreciate it, and respond in turn.

My wife had decided to buy an Acura. She was 95% certain about what she wanted. The issues were minor: What kind of trim came with certain body styles? What interior colors went with the exterior paints? A couple of questions about safety features. It was a done deal!

As we entered the showroom, we were greeted by an effusive salesman telling us how smart we were to be looking at Acuras (a variation of the dreaded "I know just what you need" opening). My wife walked over to the model of interest. The salesman stayed with me and started laying on his pitch. Thinking it might be useful for the buyer to hear some of it, I moseyed toward my wife, salesman in tow.

As she inspected the car, he took it from the top, as the media folks say, telling us every conceivable fact he could about it. My wife and I both tried to interrupt him to ask questions. He brushed every one aside with "in a minute." Having started his pitch at the rear bumper, he had reached the front door when my impatience got the better of me.

"Look, we're going to buy one – we just have a question about colors." "In a minute" was his response.

I couldn't resist it: "You're not going to let us buy until you've finished your story, are you?"

Not a blink, not a hesitation, he just kept going.

He finally allowed us to buy the car, but when we returned for service he was gone, and within a year the dealership had a new owner. The Acura is a fine product, but no dealership could survive this marketing approach.

This is a true story and it is repeated thousands of times each day. The pitch may be more subtle, but it loses sales just the same.

Try taking this test:

- Have you ever glanced up to see a prospect stifling a yawn?
- Has any prospect said, "I guess that covers it" or something similar?
- Have you heard, "But what about ..." twice or more in one of your prospect's meetings?
- Have you sometimes run out of time with your story three-quarters told?
- Did you come to the end of the meeting still showing your slides or talking through your prepared charts?
- Do you have meetings where attendees leave on you?

Answering yes to any question makes you at least an honorary member of the "in a minute" club. You're not alone. Most thoughtful, promising salespeople answer yes to at least one of those questions. If you said no to all of them, you're either one of the few top salespeople around or one of the worst. You're either simply terrific, or blind beyond belief to your customer's signals.

The trouble with scripts is that they leave no room for the unexpected, for the customer's whims or moods. Thank God that people are moody, because mood means emotion and without emotion, nobody buys. Those moods, emotions, interests, often change as you talk. Responding to these changes means sales success. The best salespeople exhibit a "risky versatility" rather than tired traditional technique.

I never made the same call twice. I had a goal for every meeting or presentation and a rough idea of how I expected to get there. But from the moment I entered the building, I was listening, looking, sensing what the atmosphere was – fear, anger, enthusiasm, apathy, confusion, preoccupation, the readiness of the client to act, the degree of warmth and intimacy I felt, whether the room was dark or bright, gloomy or cheerful, cramped or comfortable. Based on that data, I would choose a plan of action that matched the mood. And often even that simple plan would be altered as the meeting progressed.

At times I even cancelled or postponed a meeting if I saw that my prospect or client was frazzled or distracted by some actual or potential crisis. Remember, part of what you're selling (and what your customers are buying) is an awareness of their needs – personal and professional. It should be the customers that set your agenda, not your calendar or the clock.

It's the difference between a good house painter and a superb portrait painter. Both use paint, follow some similar rules – yellow and green make blue. One is doing what almost anybody can learn to do, while the other creates a result almost no one can ever equal. To the portrait painter, every subject is a unique individual and must be handled differently. In the same way, the successful sales professional sees each situation as unfolding in its own unique way. Not all the tools will be needed every time. Just because the color red is on the palette doesn't mean it must be used for every portrait. The artist/salesperson selects exactly the right tools, the colors, the theme to create a result precisely suited to the client's needs.

Selling the major account requires much more than technique. You must be seen, not as one more gray-flannel personality in a sea of forgettable nondescripts, but as yourself. Showing up, knowing your stuff, building your strengths and being ready to improvise are the keys to becoming a star in your client's eyes. And you have only yourself as the instrument. No palette, no brush, just your own wits and being.

Chapter 3
See Anybody Once

You hear so much today about qualifying prospects over the phone. Is she or he the economic buyer? Is there a budget line? Who else has to approve? The list goes on and on. It's all baloney. These days, many businesses are so complicated, reorganizations so frequent that buyers don't even know they're buyers until told. Usually by an astute seller.

Modern selling makes it worth seeing anyone once. Very few people will be buyers in the classic sense, but they will provide clues to how the world works at good old Bilge Beer. You need help – in finding the buyer, in identifying or creating the buying process, in learning who the players are. This information isn't to be found in a phone call, in Bilge's annual report or in your sales plan. It's found in the field, from talking to a lot of people.

Harry of Hanover

Twenty-five years ago, traditionalists talked about qualifying, too. It sounded great, but my trouble was a bit different. I couldn't get anybody to see me, period. I just wanted an appointment. Smarter, wiser guys could qualify. Not me. I was in trouble. My boss was putting on the heat. My job was on the line. I would see anybody who would see me.

Finally, an appointment. It didn't quite fit our client profile. I was selling, or rather *trying* to sell, consulting services to high-tech organizations with college-educated work forces – Bell Labs, IBM, Digital Equipment. This appointment was at a small factory in Hanover, Pennsylvania, which manufactured shoes and wholesaled them to big retailers. Hanover didn't seem a hotbed of desire for outside consultants. The aged gray plant surrounded by a ten-foot chain-link fence topped by barbed wire was even less promising. I trudged on, told the guard of my pending meeting with Harry. "Oh yeah, you'll find him in the hallway." Huh? "Yep."

I walked through two double doors just like those in my old high school, four- by ten-foot varnished swinging doors, opening on a long hallway that ran the length of the building. Everybody who worked in that place had to walk through that hallway and in or out those doors. It was dark, too.

About 30 feet down the hallway was a gray World War II army-issue desk with a black rubber top and a kitchen chair in front. Behind the desk, in a slightly larger wooden chair, was my Harry. Above his head, one 100-watt bulb hung from the high ceiling. The desk, light bulb and chairs were the only free-standing objects in the entire hallway. Talk about being put out to pasture! This was a lonely man.

I'd traveled a long way and he *did* add to my body count. So I took the other chair and told my story with as much enthusiasm as I could muster. It was tough. The hall echoed with my voice in the intervals between the random shift changes, coffee breaks and deliveries that were constantly filling this sound-chamber with people and chatter. At these moments, one could not speak, much less think. Finally, I ran down, out of gas and wanting more than anything else to get out of there and out of town.

Harry had said hardly a word. He'd had a vague, out-of-focus look when I arrived. I had done nothing to change it. But as I collected my things, he said, "We don't buy that kind of stuff, but Kinney Shoes might. They're over in Camp Hill. They're modern, give 'em a try." I never saw Harry or Hanover again but I did call on Kinney Shoes. They have been a client for nineteen years and at times my largest.

See anybody who will see you. Buyers are hard to find in the modern organization. You need a guide to the jungle. Maybe *this* person will be it.

An old sales adage goes like this: "Never write when you can phone. Never phone when you can meet." Relationships are built face-to-face. If there were ten commandments of modern selling, the first five would be that rule. Whether you're selling accounting services or office furniture, complexity and confusing choices force the client to make the decision based on *intangible* qualities surrounding the product. "Do I really believe I'll get the service promised?" "Is this thing really as good as she says?" "Will I look bad with this choice?" "Is it truly that simple to install?" These are "feeling" questions, which the buyer poses in his head and has to answer for himself. But the better your relationship, the more positive will be the response to your promises. *You are your product's competitive edge.* So you need to "show up" and let the buyer see the true difference between your product and that of the guy next door.

The selling process always begins with a meeting. It's at this meeting that you determine if an individual is a prospect or not. Your first phone call to the target is not to screen, but to make an appointment. The phone does *not* work either to clarify your product or service or to identify key prospect issues. Politics will be involved in every purchase. Also, people buy for personal reasons. Nobody talks about this sort of thing on the phone, especially to strangers. For that matter, why tell much of anything to a stranger?

A major part of your success will be due to the number of first calls you make. One of every seven turns into business within the first year. Appointments matter. If you don't have a plan for them, it's unlikely you'll ever have a client base capable of generating big dollars for you.

Getting Names

Obviously, the way to get an appointment is to start with a good name – and that can be difficult. Existing customers are always good sources. Asking for references can get you a name *and* often surface new needs with that customer, too. Never ask for a referral cold. Describe the ideal client or the ideal issue. In effect, tell a story, excite your existing client's brain cells, then ask for the referral.

However, you may be low on your organization's totem pole and have no clients as yet. In that case, make a list of 40 accounts (non-clients) you want to do business with in the next year or two. Get the best names you can but don't expect much. Many experienced salespeople get caught in a trap when cold-calling. They get a name, they call, they try to set something up. If it fails, they find another name. This is a horrible time waster. You should build a "critical mass" of names before you start – at least 50. This helps in two ways. First, your phone time is better organized and second, you get stronger after every phone call you make. Take advantage of this by making a bunch of calls at one time.

Call each one for an appointment. If you're selling ground maintenance and the person on the other end of the line works in computer research, don't give up. Ask whom *they* think you should call. Call that person and tell them so-and-so in computer science thinks they may be the person you should be talking to.

With the advent of voice-mail, you are bound to have a lot of one-way "conversations." Simply asking for a call back can make you very lonely. Write out a commercial – a 20-second spot – and read it into the machine. You're trying to sell an appointment. Give somebody a reason to return your call. Don't wait for something to happen, make it happen.

Finally, a suspect! Be brief. Tell who you are, who you represent. State the issues and problems your product addresses. Ask if these are issues of interest to him or her. If so, you'd like to meet to tell your story, learn more about their situation and determine if further discussion makes sense. State that this first meeting is exploratory. Ask for a 30-minute appointment. Don't expect it to be offered. Be prepared to ask twice.

Some pointers to note:

- Stand up while telephoning. You will automatically modulate your voice. You will come across with more energy and force. You will 'show up' better.

- Don't sell. It can't be done on the phone.
- Don't screen. That is one purpose of the first meeting.
- Have alternative days and times available. If you must travel to get there, have two trips blocked out so you can provide a back-up alternative.
- After agreement on an appointment, suggest that others can be invited to the meeting.
- Start the relationship in a professional way: confirm the appointment in writing, using a simple standard letter.

Computeritis

Every now and then a salesperson will be attacked by a virus called computeritis. It's not fatal, but it can turn a star into an also-ran in a hurry. The salesperson wants to "get organized." Clients, prospects, deadbeats, notes, gossip, data of all kinds are input into the computer program. Travel schedules, lists of people to call today, things to do are spewed out. "Ah," the salesperson thinks, "I've got my act together."

One of my salesmen had a nearly fatal attack of computeritis. A prospect would call from out of state. He was interested. He would like to do something. My salesman would consult his screen, inform the prospect that he planned to be in his area in a couple of weeks. See you then!

My guy was trying to sell on *his* schedule. His disease made him forget that people buy on their own schedule. His job was to respond to the client *at that moment*, not find a way to fit him into his plan.

Computer data is no substitute for a paper copy of important accounts and phone numbers. You just might be looking at that list over a cup of coffee and think, "What the hell, let's give Sam a call." Maybe it's ESP or something in the air, but good things come about more frequently from that kind of spontaneous action than statistics say they should. Who knows – maybe you carry a more casual, relaxed attitude in the random action. In any event, it works. Stars always give chance a chance.

The Good, The Bad, and the Ugly

People often sound like buyers, talk like buyers, smell like buyers, and act like buyers. Later to our dismay, we discover they ain't buyers and, if the truth be known, never will be. What's going on here? Part of the answer is that very few people want to say, "I can't buy." In a perverse way, they believe it's the same as saying, "I'm powerless; others direct me." So they talk big and act little. And if you call them on it, you make them look bad. So much for *that* relationship.

Since you will see anybody once, it's best to think of all the people you meet as contacts rather than prospects. Fortunately, contacts will quickly sort themselves out.

The Good

Good prospects show up easily. They talk trouble – "Six key computer programmers quit in a huff over our new rotating-shift policy" – rather than general needs like increasing productivity and improving communications. You can always "see" trouble; its a story with people in it. A need only becomes trouble when people are involved. I've got a television set in my basement. It works, but it's not connected to the cable system. You might say I have a need. That's true, but I only decided to pay for the cable hook-up when my daughter started exercising in the basement and complained she couldn't watch her favorite programs. Then I had trouble!

The Kinda Good – The Shopper

This is a person who wants to know all about your product; says that he likes it a lot; that it meets real needs; that he would like to know more – but somehow action never happens. A shopper is looking, never buying. It's a way to appear powerful. Shoppers feel good when they're shopping. Those "shop-till-I-drop" T-shirts and the people in them aren't kidding.

Shoppers are like teddy bears. It's nice to have one or two to keep you company, but who needs hundreds? And if you don't let go you'll have hundreds. They're friendly, chatty, warm and they will watch you slowly starve to death from lack of sales. They can fill your day, every day.

Identifying and letting go of shoppers is one of the keys to sales success. It's not hard to identify one. First, your gut tells you loud and clear. Second, shoppers always talk vague needs, never trouble.

If you're suspicious, here is a test: Ask "If I had a pill that everyone could take to make this problem go away, and it costs X dollars for each pill, would you or your company buy, and how many?" This is the "go away" pill. If you can't sell this hypothetical pill, you've got a shopper.

Shoppers also like to meet alone. If you can't seem to meet any other people, you've got a shopper.

There is nothing evil about shoppers; they're mostly nice people. They're just doing their job-looking. Stay loosely connected. Include them in the Good category. Keep them on your mailing list. Phone once in a while. Ask for referrals. By the way, you'll get some. Shoppers often become conspirators and/or champions who will guide you to somebody who has some pain.

The Bad

This is the naysayer, a guy who wants to puncture every balloon. This person is usually a BUMP (barely upward mobile professional) who is sure he can do it cheaper, better and always winds up doing nothing at all. Change has to be stopped. Evolution was a hot idea but enough's enough. He has no problems, at least none that he's aware of. Your stuff looks good, but expensive.

Often salespeople will work hard to turn someone like this into a prospect – that is, someone with a problem and a desire to do something about it. The would-be seller counsels, teaches, cajoles, flatters, sells and sells. This can take months, even years. But it's like trying to teach a pig to sing: it wastes your time and annoys the pig.

Finally, sometimes, the person says, "You're right. I do have a need, so now I'd better look around." Yep, you made a sale of sorts, you convinced them they should do something. They bought that idea, now they're looking for alternatives. Often they end up buying from somebody else. You've become comfortable, familiar, the excitement is gone. (Remember, people buy with their hearts.) So Brand X is new, different. It looks as if it meets the need you created. They buy it and look to you for an "attaboy."

Sales professionals are divided in their feelings about naysayers. Some dislike them; others hate them.

Don't waste your time with them. Fold your tent, close your case and vamoose. Your job is finding prospects, not making them! Seeing lots of people and selling meetings is the way to *find* prospects. Leave conversions to the religious. They're looking for business, too.

The Ugly

It's the first call. You've barely opened your mouth and the contact says, "This sounds good, great, terrific. This is just what we need, where have you been? We'll need hundreds, thousands, millions."

You're dead. This guy can't buy anything, never has bought anything, has no intention of buying – and if by some chance you find a true prospect in his company, Ugly will do all he can to kill the deal.

These folks give themselves away early. They always tell one or more of the Four Fibs:

- "Money is no problem."
- "My boss approves anything I want."
- "I know all about your stuff."
- "I'm in charge."

None of them is ever true. As the old adage goes: "When they tell you it's not the money, it's the money!" *If it sounds too good to be true, believe me, it isn't true!*

Follow up quickly on the Good. Stay in touch with the Shoppers. They won't all become hot prospects, but they will help with referrals and give you good press. As for the Bad and the Ugly, leave them for the other salespeople. They need something to occupy their time.

Chapter 4
Pink Smoke

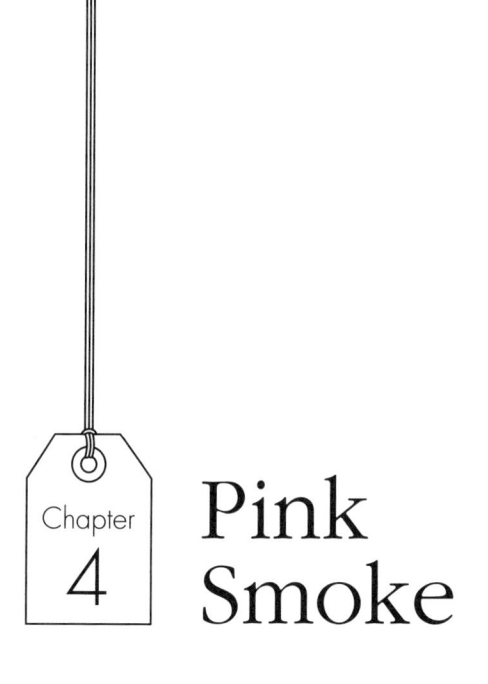

What do you do for a living? Like most major-account salespeople, I never had a short answer to the question. The actual product – that combination of things, delivery and promises I sold – varied from client to client. My attempts at explanation grew long-winded, more obfuscating than clarifying, frustrating to me and, I'm sure, to others. There was simply no way to describe in a few words the complex, subtle, exciting, everchanging job of the professional salesperson. When asked, I responded: "I sell pink smoke." I rarely got a follow-up question.

Pink smoke? It's there in every sales situation – those indefinite, mysterious, elusive aspects, things you can't see or know for sure. Your relationship with the buyer is critical, but how do you define it? Many sales turn on the unexpected, on serendipity, a shock. You never make the same sale twice, there is always something a little different. What part did your enthusiasm play in making it happen? One thing for sure, selling is full of surprises. Most of what happens to make a sale can't be seen or measured.

What am I selling? What is the customer buying? These are extraordinarily difficult questions to answer in a big-ticket sale. Just what is contained in the total "package" the buyer(s) bought? What kind of personal and professional profit do they expect as a result of the purchase?

And, of course, the "Three Cs" of modern business – Change, Complexity and Choice – are always at work to shuffle buyers, requirements and priorities as the selling cycle ambles along.

Ah, for the simpler days of single product, problem, answer and buyer. Then a product or service did one or two tasks. It often solved just one problem. The old grocery cash register of 40 years ago kept track of the money and provided a receptacle to hold it. End of story. Now we have POS (point of sale) systems which perform the old cash register tasks, but in addition, do inventory control, market research, order stock, spot buying trends, make price changes, identify peak shopping times, and schedule the workforce. POS systems are intricate devices connected to every other part of the corporation.

A major-account salesperson walks into a prospect's office without a well-defined "thing" to sell. Generally, you have a core item or service around which you add bells, whistles, terms, financing, official and unofficial commitments, guarantees, redesign for special needs. Every *customer* wants a *custom* job.

One might think a jet engine is about as tangible as a product can get. However, no airline has bought a jet engine off the shelf for years. The final contracts discuss finances, services, mechanical modifications, buy backs, and run to hundreds of pages. Not to mention that political issues may affect the deal. For example, should British Airways buy a U.S. made General Electric engine or a domestically manufactured Rolls Royce?

There is no such thing as a tangible product now. Everybody sells intangibles. We live in the white water of rapid, unanticipated change, growing complexity and technology run amok. As the sources of manufacturing, the methods of distribution, the variety of forms a product can take multiply, buying the product or service is just a small part of the purchase. Will it arrive in time? Will it work as I expect? Can I get service? Good answers to these questions become as important as the product itself.

Take Me Out to the Ball Game

Let's go to the ball game: Crosley Field in Cincinnati, 1960. It was a small park – 28,000 seats – for the Cincinnati Reds. (It was torn down a few years later, replaced by Riverfront Stadium.) As you entered the old place, you could see the hot dogs boiling in vats. The stockyard was less than a half mile away. As the game began, the familiar cry "Get your Red Hot here!" was heard around the field. Red Hots were sold by mostly middle-aged men moonlighting from other jobs. When you bought that hot dog you were buying a tangible product. You knew enough about your world – downtown Cincinnati – and how it worked to make some pretty good assumptions about your purchase.

Fast forward 30 years. Riverfront Stadium. You still hear the cry "Get your Red Hot here!" But where did that wiener come from? Is it local, or shipped from Mexico or even further? Is it chicken, turkey, beef, or some weird unnamed concoction? Is it going to be hot? Where did they heat it inside this giant complex? How long has it been in storage? And where did that strange looking vendor with the long, greasy hair come from? My God, he's scary. The complications of modern life have turned a known quantity into something less sure. That "Red Hot" has become an intangible.

And the promises of that vendor that your hot dog is indeed "red hot," fresh, or all beef become suspect. When did he get this job? Possibly only moments before you sat down. Does he even know what's in the box he carries? Was the box recently off-loaded from a truck bringing it from a distant site?

That hot dog vendor at the ball park is selling as much promise – "Get your Red Hot here!" – as product. You expect that frank to be hot, but there's no reliable way to test that assumption in advance. So you fork over a couple of bucks and hope. Hot dogs, hair styling, hardware, health care are more intangible than tangible. Some products, like hot dogs, can't be tested before purchase. Others also depend on the delivery. Only the mirror will tell you if that perm is what you wanted. Systems, such as health care, need to run smoothly over time to prove their worth.

A modern world filled with choice provides numerous options to a buyer and complexity makes delivery critical, be it hot dogs or health care. As we all know, if it can go wrong, it will. When you buy a car, service is never far from your mind. Promises may be contractual or guaranteed, but paper is still paper. It can't make a delivery happen. It can't make a hot dog hot. It can't provide the towing service on a cold night. Only people can keep a promise.

We live in a complex world where nothing can be easily fixed. Remember the quaint, not too distant past when homeowners could repair their washer or tune the family auto! When something goes wrong today you need an expert. (Even then, who knows. When my electronic phone died, a call to the manufacturer's service rep in Tennessee brought this advice: "Lift it up three inches and drop it!")

Today, product and delivery are seen as one purchase. A product is really a "thing" plus delivery. Maintenance, implementation, installation, service, follow-up are just other words for delivery. And delivery can't be assured in advance. The customer, like you at the ball game, has only promises. Whether the customer believes those promises depends on how much the seller is trusted.

Some sales theorists would like you to believe that every sale is only an economic transaction. To them a hot dog is just a wiener. If you're only buying a hot dog, you may decide to take your chances with that scruffy-looking vendor. Maybe. But if you're buying something more expensive or important, something you will be using for a while, you get a lot more interested in the seller.

Your Product is You

Firing a loyal, honest, likeable guy is most unpleasant. I felt terrible. But his misdeed was the worst; I had no choice. He couldn't keep his promises. Oh, his intentions were good. He'd make an appointment for 8:00 a.m. and show up at 8:30. Reports, letters, actions were late, incorrect or superficially done. There was always a bumbling banality about his excuses – the plane was delayed, a flu attack, an auto accident.

How could anybody buy from him? Promises were at least half the product he was selling. Clients would only get half or less of what they paid for. And they knew it!

The product in *every* big deal is largely promises. Official promises of delivery, quality, maintenance, services, follow-up, etc. And, of course, unofficial promises.

Here's how one salesperson lost out. She sold a software financial package to a buyer in Johnston City, Tennessee. The training and orientation for the system was scheduled for San Francisco. Both buyer and seller knew the buyer wanted to go to San Francisco as much or more than he wanted the software. The venue was changed to Atlanta. Our seller let her secretary tell the buyer. She was all too aware that she was not delivering on the personal purchase. The buyer's expectations were not met and he felt an injustice had been done. Yep, the buyer went to Atlanta and bought the software, the last software he would ever buy from her. She made a promise and didn't keep it.

In most major-account sales, the *product* is a bundling of the technical expertise and professional skills of your organization plus your promises.

PRODUCT OR SERVICE = CUSTOMIZED CORE "THING" + PROMISES

Whether a promise is official or unofficial doesn't matter. Both are equally parts of the contract. The saleswoman didn't deliver the total purchase. She knew it. That's why she had the secretary call. But since the trip to San Francisco wasn't written in the specifications, she thought she could renege. She was wrong. Unless she accepts that any promise she makes is a professional commitment she is destined for mediocrity.

"Total Quality" is the latest hot idea for achieving corporate success. In sales, total quality is easy; you achieve it by keeping your promises. Not some, not many, not only the official ones, but *all* of them. A broken promise is a defect. You're selling a package of product and promise and you will be responsible for delivering all of what you sell. A failed promise is like a blown engine in a new Mercedes. It is never forgotten. Never! Even if people say they have. They haven't. Ever.

Hearing a promise and believing in one are two very different things. I can hear anyone's promise, but I believe only the promises of those I trust. I don't trust strangers and I don't trust people I don't like. I do trust people with whom I have a good relationship. Put another way:

$$\boxed{\text{PRODUCT OR SERVICE}} = \boxed{\text{CUSTOMIZED CORE "THING"}} + \boxed{\text{RELATIONSHIP}}$$

No Relationship, No Sale

You don't say "trust me" and have people trust you. You earn trust. The way to earn trust is by keeping your promises. Bit by bit, your prospects and clients begin to believe in a most important sales promise: "I will make you look good!" If you can't keep the little promises you make during the selling process, e.g., if you're late for meetings, if you present incomplete proposals, if you show insensitivity to the customer's needs, there's no need to worry about the big promise. You've already run up "No Sale" on your cash register.

Building Alliances

The word relationship has twelve letters, but most people think it's a four-letter word. It's hard to think of a word falling into disrepute faster. And with good reason. Lots of folks are "into relationships" or "in a relationship." People who talk the most about relationships seem to know the least. A relationship language exists: authenticity, bonding, sharing, respecting someone's space, connecting, et al. We've all heard the words. They have that tinny, thin, hollow ring. We suspect, perhaps unfairly, that the speaker just can't be trusted. No real person talks like that! At least nobody we want to be connected with. Yet building a relationship with your buyer means sales success. More than that – no relationship, no sale!

One measure of relationship quality is the number of things we can easily talk about:

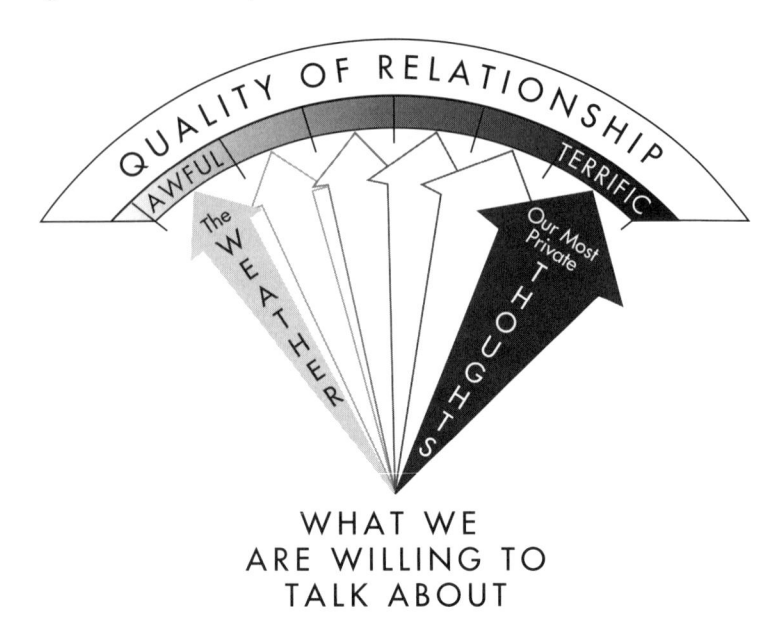

QUALITY OF RELATIONSHIP
AWFUL — TERRIFIC
The Weather — Our Most Private Thoughts

WHAT WE
ARE WILLING TO
TALK ABOUT

But how do you achieve an easy rapport with another person? What are the makings of a good relationship? Without the trite expressions, without the phony honesty, that's a tough question! Most of the words we like to use are ruined by misuse, but I can tell you what I want from a relationship. Help me feel better about myself, wiser, more powerful, on the right track. Be enthusiastic; give the impression that all things are possible and easy. Give me courage. Spend time with me; be sensitive to my moods. If I'm in bad shape, give me a break. Listen to me – pay attention – no matter how crazy; it matters to me. Take that extra step for me.

You can't be a winner at everything, but you should be an expert in your product and your field. You ought to be able to state my problem more clearly than I can. Clear thinking is part of what I'm buying. If you can't, get out of sales. I won't buy from someone who brings more ambiguity to my life.

New facts should stretch my awareness, vision, expectations. I should say, "I've been forced to rethink some of my ideas." "You helped me see the problem in a new way." Insights can be delivered in other ways, too; a fresh idea about my career, a bit of news about other clients, about the world you see everyday and I don't.

Can you laugh at yourself? Are you witty? Do you really, really know at the bottom the world is mad? Can you laugh, period? Do you believe work can be funny? Do you know moods move me? Do you know that the sale is an emotional event, not a rational one? Do you know I buy for personal reasons more than business reasons? Can you do something wacky? Unexpected? If you answered no to any question (how *could* you?), think about it! If you can't be fun or funny, go into the funeral business.

Accept me as an equal partner, not as a dink to be manipulated. See me as a person, not just a money machine. Remember, you can't fake this. You can say the right words, but the body doesn't lie. Your words are rumors. Your tone, intonation, timing, body language, pauses, rhythm, silence tell the real truth. To really give me consideration means face-to-face meetings and frequent phone contact. Absence does not make the heart grow fonder.

As you can see, relationship-building is no small task. Living life might seem simple, but relationships are not. The consequences of insensitivity can be embarrassment, humiliation or anger. Developing a good relationship is definitely not something any damn fool can do easily.

You arrive as a stranger at the start of your relationship with a client. But you must instill certain basic premises right from the beginning:

- I am genuinely interested in you
- I am here to help you be successful
- I am added value (technical knowledge)
- I will always go the extra mile for you
- I will not take advantage of the relationship (until I've earned the right!)

Before you can put these notions across with any sincerity, you must have the right attitude toward customers. You must believe that they are human beings like yourself, living life the only way they know, experiencing the same fears, anxieties and concerns you have. Here's a test to determine whether you've established a relationship with someone: Can you sense yourself in the other person? Once you begin to see something of yourself in another, you can no longer look on that person as a stranger. Like it or not, a bond has been formed.

Walk Tall

Much is said about sellers becoming partners with buyers. The sad reality is that most buyer/seller relationships are dependent. Me Chief, you Indian. I'm the boss, you're the flunky. I believe this cycle is established by the seller. If you feel uncertain about the value of your profession, that gets communicated to buyers, who, all too happily, assume the superior role given to them. If you let prospects tell you how to act, what to say, what to do and when to do it, forget making sales, you're not even making friends.

There is never any reason to be obsequious. Life is too short; selling is too important. Without sales, this world would wind down in a hurry. Making a market is the key to economic growth. Not many people truly believe they would be happier harvesting berries, clothed in animal hides and living in mud huts.

The role you see for yourself places a boundary on the relationship. *To be treated as a colleague, you must act like one.* Behaving as a child tends to bring out the parent in everyone else. Your role as seller should always encompass that of friend, supporter, confidant, peer.

Three is a Magic Number

Relationships are built through frequency of contact. You need to see people a number of times in different circumstances. You can't build a relationship with someone you've only seen once. You can't fax a handshake. It is the *number* of meetings/visits/lunches/phone calls that count, not the length of each encounter.

For example, when two people meet at a social event and they hit it off, one will likely say, "Let's have drinks or dinner next week." Out of a series of more or less formal meetings, a relationship might develop. It's not just the meetings that count. The time intervals between them are equally or maybe even more important. People need to think through and reflect on the most recent meeting. It's through this process that they become aware of the questions they need to ask or behavior they want to observe at the next get-together.

What's true in social settings is true for sales calls as well. You're talking to see if it's worth meeting again. A relationship is built out of a number of interactions. An interaction is a face-to-face meeting. Occasionally a telephone call works. Letters don't count.

Just assume you're in a social setting. Don't monopolize the conversation. Be interested in the other person. Disclose something personal about yourself. Ask to meet again. Think about how to move forward in the relationship.

You need at least three meetings to establish a relationship with another person, and you probably need three relationships in an organization before a prospect becomes a client.

Put Yourself in Their Shoes

When you hear bad news from the client, don't just think: How does this affect me? Or how does this affect the deal? Think: How does this affect my client? Helping a prospect avoid a mistake or hasty judgment makes everybody look good. A great test question for any action you plan to request: Would you ask your son or daughter to do this? Do what you know is right.

Put yourself in the other person's shoes. If you were the client, would you say yes to your request? This doesn't mean you only ask people to do easy things. It does mean you don't ask someone to do something you wouldn't do. If you would ask for advice before making the commitment, tell the prospect they should get advice.

One of my saleswomen had the opportunity to present our services to a conference of European managers of a major international company. The director from Spain was interested. He'd like to give it a test. A test was $20,000 or so. He was comfortable and committed. My saleswoman was uneasy. Should she push for more? "Would it make sense for the director?" I asked. "Not really" was the reply. "Then forget it – wait a couple of months, let them get started, then go to Spain." That visit was more than the manager expected. Their relationship was solid. Yes, he wanted more, $85,000 more, and he wanted to introduce the program to the rest of Europe for her.

Be around when the client/prospect needs help. Former President Nixon's Attorney General John Mitchell said in the Seventies: "When the going gets tough, the tough get going." In the ego-maniacal Eighties, that would be rephrased: "When the going gets tough, the tough split." Hopefully the Nineties will say: "When the going gets tough, count on me." Always take the extra step. Relationships *only* become exceptional when at least one party delivers more than the minimal expectation.

Take Time for a Tiger

Anthony Burgess, in his famous novel on colonial Malaya, *The Long Day Wanes*, described a British officer, who when faced with any local dispute always suggested that the parties "take time for a Tiger." He frequently joined the group for more than a few "Tigers." Tiger was and is the most popular local beer in Malaysia. The advice is still as good as the beer.

Schedule a meeting without objectives. Relationships are two-way streets. You need to hear the other guy's agenda, the personal and/or professional concerns he's worried about, aspires to, hopes for or just plain obsesses on. Try asking: How are you doing? What are your plans? How is the job, family? This takes time. The Earl of Chesterfield said over a hundred years ago, "Many a man would rather you heard his story than solved his problem." Still true today. You can't devote five minutes to the other person's agenda then run on for 45 more about your anxiety, namely getting the business, and expect to succeed.

Take a Chance

Now for the tough part. A relationship cannot be strictly intellectual. That is a cold connection and people get wary. They want an emotional bond as well. They want you to think about *and* feel for them. That requires some disclosure of your feelings and fears and, of course, that's a big risk. You're vulnerable, but taking a chance of this kind both builds and reflects trust. Very few people are willing to take this kind of chance, so most connections are never more than acquaintanceships. When you are forming a relationship, a measure of self-disclosure is what separates the automaton from the artist.

Building a relationship with your customer is the most powerful sales idea you'll ever get. A personal relationship between buyer and seller is the river on which your commerce flows. There float the barges of product and services you sell. No river, no barge moves. Salespeople almost always sell too soon, they talk barges when no river exists to carry the freight.

In a complex, changing universe you must have solid, deep, connected relationships. Without them, who will believe your promises? Who will tell you of an opportunity? Who will be your guide? Your champion? Who will buy from you? People buy with their heads *and* their hearts. A hot dog is *never* just another wiener.

Chapter 5: Selling the Goat

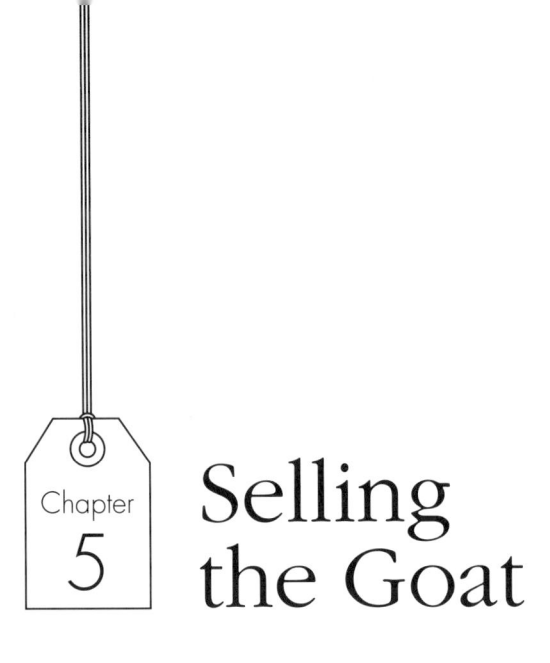

Imagine this situation. You have a mountain goat for sale. It's your first call on a new account. "What are you selling?" Albert asks, so you show him the goat. "Look at that fur. Fur like that can handle temperatures to 50 degrees below zero. Check those hooves. Notice how delicate they are. This goat can handle any crack or crevice. This goat doesn't burn many calories so if vegetation is sparse or under snow, he'll still make it. Notice the center of gravity. This goat can handle any weather. No chance of losing this one in a big storm." Bit by bit, Albert is intrigued. "It is a furry little thing, ain't it." He likes what he sees and tells you so. Sound familiar? It should. We've all tried to sell that goat at one time or another.

But what if Albert had never seen a mountain range, valleys, cliffs, ledges, or rock falls. Why did he buy your goat? He doesn't know what to do with it. He only bought it out of curiosity. "Oh well, I'll buy one and see what happens."

That's the worst thing that could happen to a salesperson. Yes, you have a customer. A customer who just bought his last goat. He sees your goat as a curio, not a solution.

Even worse, now that he's living with it, he thinks he knows more about what your goat can do than you. You're no longer in control of the sales cycle. You can bet the client will do less business than you plan for. Always. He will do bad things to and with your goat, then complain about the lousy goats you sell.

Your job on the first call is not to sell goats. Your job is to describe the mountain range – that is, define prospect problems so effectively that the prospect says, "You know, we need something up on that ledge there." *Then* you show the goat!

Every product or service is seen only as a forlorn goat until you clearly describe the client world of problems and opportunities for which your product is an answer. In other words, every product is just a goat until the issues it solves are on the table.

Are you selling a product (the goat) or solving a problem? That question will elicit a flinch from any salesperson who has been around the block and the reflexive answer will be: "I solve customer problems!" Well they got the answer right, but how come there is so much goat dung all over their shoes. And what's that smell!

Look, we've all sold that goat. We know better, yet we do it. Why? Why do we dump all that product detail on the first call, often to bored, uninterested non-buyers?

The reasons are complex, but worth exploring. After all, if we persist in taking the least effective action, the answer can't be simple. There are at least three reasons why we trot out that goat on the first call.

It's FABulous

We may be selling goat because it's the only thing we know how to do. We were trained in the "product push" school. This is the classic features, advantages, benefits (FAB) approach. Another aspect of this strategy is "Let's be friends; you scratch my back, I'll scratch yours." In effect, goat plus a friendly goat herder. It clearly works. Nothing is sold without a good relationship between buyer and seller, but it's easy to become cynical about the customer. A big-ticket item purchased without a clear connection to an organizational need will soon be challenged. Except for small-ticket, low-consequence purchases, selling the goat is a sure prescription for a new career.

Meeting the Demand

Every experienced salesperson has heard about the dangers in selling and showing product features too early. Salespeople react to this advice much like Marvin "Bad News" Barnes did to coaching. Bad News was a pro basketball player for the Detroit Pistons. Bad News had a bad habit. Every time he got the ball, he shot it! (Like a salesperson selling features on every call.) As you might imagine, this practice made Detroit a low-scoring team. Finally, according to a report in the *Detroit Free Press*, the coach couldn't take it any longer. He confronted Bad News. "Look Marvin, you're taking too many shots. It's ruining the team." Bad News responded, "I know, I know. I don't want to, but my fans be demanding it."

Selling product first is like shooting those hoops. Salespeople can't resist showing product features because our first few contacts in a company seem to be demanding it. The more technical our response, the better. They want to see that goat down to the last detail. That's because these folks are usually feasibility buyers. The economic buyer – the person with the problem and the money – has delegated the job of answering the question "Sounds good, but will it work?" to them. Their job is to determine whether the solution that we propose will work. These are the people we meet at the first call. They're "buying" all right, but not what we're selling. We are selling solutions to organizational problems. They're looking for features (the goat). Their question is always "How does it work?"

Now you're stuck. Answer the question (show the goat) and you've made your contact an "expert" on your product or service. They'll feel they're prepared to present your case to the economic buyer. Now you're really a "goner" because the economic buyer is looking for an answer, not a goat. You've just created some lousy goat salespeople who will do your job more poorly than you ever dreamed possible.

No one can tell your story as well as you can and nobody can convey that you keep your promises, that you're someone to be trusted. Remember, a product is a "thing" *plus* your promises. There is simply no way they can represent your total product effectively.

I'll Ask the Questions Around Here

In the 1970s, we began to replace the old-time religion – the product push – with a new one: the consultative approach. We sought to identify customer needs through diagnostic questions and prescribe solutions.

Unfortunately, it's very rare for a seller to encounter the economic buyer – the person with the pain and the answers – right away. Most early client contacts are feeling no pain and have few answers. They're gathering information, checking the feasibility of your alternative, or just plain shopping. They rarely know the extent of the problem or its true priority.

Nobody forms a good relationship by asking people questions they can't answer. You may make people appear impotent, uninformed and stupid. Not quite the way to put your best foot forward. I'm not against asking questions and I certainly want all the account information I can get, but questions should be a tool, not a rule. And, in fact, they are more useful at subsequent meetings and presentations.

Further, the consultative approach assumes a doctor/patient relationship between seller and buyer. That's a risky assumption. I've only met a few salespeople who had the "weight" to carry that off in the first call. Such a relationship is even more unlikely when a seller (even a good one) is in a new job. And it is almost never established with a young salesperson. People just don't answer questions of those who haven't established their credentials. We salespeople don't have M.D. behind our names; we have to create our reputation. Probing questions can often seem impertinent early in the relationship. Prospects want to know "Who are you?" "Why should I listen?" "Why spend time answering questions if I don't have any idea of your capability?"

What's worse, prospects will interrupt the diagnosis and demand, "Okay, okay, so what's your story?" They demand information and pretty soon here comes that horned, bearded ruminant into view.

The Issues Start

So what's the alternative? How do you handle that first meeting without selling the goat? Every sales star opens with issues, not product. They put "value" on the table early. They start with a brief description of four or five organizational issues and problems your contact is likely to be dealing with that your product or service most effectively solves. This is what I call an *Issues Start.*

Contacts are unlikely to confide their real problems right away, but as you describe organizational issues with clarity and insight, they may be willing to acknowledge problems you have already touched upon. "These are the problems we solve; if you have one, let's talk further," is infinitely more credible than "Tell me your troubles and I'll give you the answers." Further, the "Tell me your troubles ..." approach can really backfire. The president of a Colorado property management firm told me: "I can't stand this approach and I get it all the time. *There is nothing more annoying* and it does not build credibility or trust. If I tell you my problems, of course you will tell me that your product is the best at solving them."

You create interest in your product by talking about the contact's own issues, not simply working an all-too-predictable sales track. Talking issues begins to build that mountain range, that broader context in which your product or service is most effective.

All too often, sellers neglect to set the stage. They get some sort of positive reinforcement from a prospect and away they go – trying to make that sale. Occasionally they succeed, but it's usually small potatoes with no re-order in sight. Far better to persuade the prospect that the issues you deal with are important and worth responding to. If you get agreement on the big picture, your ultimate sale will be bigger and more profitable.

The Source of Issues

There's no need to get wrapped around your axle defining what an "issue" is in precise terms. An issue is a situation your customer – potential or actual – is, or should be, concerned about and for which you have an answer. It will be some unsettled matter, a vital question that needs to be considered, a problem or concern, an opportunity.

For example, an issue could be:

- "Onerous new Federal reporting regulations require quicker compilation of personnel data"
- "The need to instill a customer service attitude in all employees"
- "An advertising message that is too diffuse"
- "Having to reduce energy costs by ten percent"
- "Trying to motivate people during a gradual reduction in the workforce"

In an actual sales call, the issues would be presented in more detail, usually with an anecdote describing the dire consequences of inaction.

Identifying issues is not hard. One simple way is to think about your products/services, then ask yourself (and colleagues if need be):

- "What organizational problems do we solve?"
- "What opportunities does a prospect organization have that we can help exploit?"

- "What problems do my customers face that my product/service can fix?"
- "What do we do better than anyone else in our field?"

A little horse sense and some creativity will give you plenty of issues. The problem is not finding issues, it's recognizing the need to look for them in the first place. Far too many salespeople are willing to let their prospects discover on their own what the product/service will do for them. Mediocre salespeople passively wait for that connection to be made.

Some of the most potent issues come from your unique vision of how the world works. More about world views in Chapter 14. For now, it is enough to say that talking about your approach, your philosophy, your framework, your paradigm, your point of view creates the most energy in a prospect. It is this information and only this information that sets you apart from the pack.

POWER TALK – A CASE STUDY

Let's watch a professional start putting these ideas together. The following story is based on actual experience.

"Bob Johnson" has joined The Bergerac Company in Dallas.* Their key product is Power Talk – a two-day seminar which dramatically improves personal presentation skills. He's been through the program. He likes it and believes it is better than competing programs. He respects the people he'll be working with and thinks the sales job will be exciting and fun.

*The Bergerac Company, 8100 Lomo Alto, Suite 200, Dallas TX 75225

After a few days he's discovered, as we all do with a new job, that things aren't quite as hot as he thought. First, everybody talks goat – all the neat little bits of seminar business – on every call. Second, prospects agree that improving presentation skills is a good idea, but it sure ain't on the top of their list of things to do. Third, there is a lot of entrenched competition out there – Communispond, Executive Technique, to name just two. Finally, when he talks to prospects, they don't perceive much difference between Power Talk, the competition, Dale Carnegie, or their own in-house creations. HELP!

Bob started by taking a hard look at the seminar itself. What did he like about it? Power Talk emphasized being more theatrical, giving more emotional presentations than the competition. Power Talk also de-emphasized rules – the touch, talk, turn mechanics so common in other programs. These features seemed to make better sense to Bob than more traditional approaches.

But why should these features, these emphases, make more sense now, he wondered. What's really going on in today's world? For one thing, people have shorter attention spans. The one-hour drone speech is dead. Ministers who used to talk for hours now preach in ten-minute "bites." Bob also had plenty of experiences in other companies where 15 agenda minutes dwindled to just five or even three. It seemed as if everyone involved in making presentations griped about the lack of time. And even worse, they hated the surprises they got at presentation time – the wrong people, too many people, a different objective, the demand that "this better be good," followed by a dire look.

Then came the insight. The world had changed. Time frames were shorter. Television had brought higher standards for presentation skills. Drama was in demand. Even meetings with set agendas weren't immune to all the change going on in the world. Power Talk was responding to this, but without really knowing why.

Now Bob knew how to build the mountain range for his goat. The issue was that people are being asked to give high priority, high impact, high consequence presentations in unrealistic time frames to audiences with a low, unpredictable threshold for boredom. All his prospects had this problem. They could feel it, see it occurring, and in many cases it had personally happened to them.

Power Talk's emphasis on "letting it all hang out," of melding theatrical skills with traditional presentation skills, made presenters more appealing to modern audiences. Power Talk's de-emphasis on rules allowed the presenter to modify his or her approach if necessary.

Bob still has a lot to work on, but now he knows how to make Power Talk unique. He has reflected on how the world works and how his product fits into that world. He has the beginnings of a philosophy for The Bergerac Company. In effect, he's answering the questions "What does The Bergerac Company believe about how the world works?" and "How do the Bergerac products meet a need in that world?"

Soon his sales calls will reflect a deeper understanding of "what's really happening out there." If he's right, prospects will agree: "You've put your finger right on it!" "That is just how it works!" And when the prospect says, "That makes sense, how do you deal with it?" a hoof or a horn is in order.

Successful sales professionals get the broader issues and problems that their product/service deals with on the table at the first meeting. The person they're meeting with won't have all the details, but will have a general awareness of the concerns that were the impetus for the meeting.

Moreover, they never show the complete goat at the first meeting. They do only enough to meet the contact's demands. If pressed, they suggest that a second meeting would be required to cover it in sufficient detail and, naturally, if we're going to go to this effort why not invite others?

And they never leave this first meeting without showing how their product or service can resolve at least one issue or problem under discussion.

Every top salesperson I've worked with knows that this universe and the people in it are complex systems. And like all complex systems, are reluctant to change. To deal with that reluctance, they talk issues and problems first. They know you can't be a consultant until somebody cares about the problem. They tell colorful stories of trouble and opportunity. They talk about people getting worse or getting better. Through an Issues Start, they add the energy necessary to get the sales process moving.

Chapter 6: Getting to First Base

It's often remarked that all sales stars are "great closers." I've got my doubts. I've known more than a few top performers who were not considered strong closers, but I've never worked with a superstar who wasn't a "great opener." They all created interest and energy at the *first* appointment with a contact. They always got something moving. I'm convinced they sold more because they got more started to begin with. Their best show was their first face-to-face contact with the prospect. You can't score if you don't get to first base.

Most everyone will subscribe to the importance of the first call. Nevertheless, so-so salespeople simply go through the motions. They're waiting for a happy accident, i.e., a genuine prospect to appear, but generally none shows up and the meeting ends with a weather report – maybe fair, maybe rain – and some luke-warm fuzzies: "Well, it sounds interesting" (the kiss of death); "If you're back this way, maybe you could stop by;" "Let me look it over and call you." A routine follow-up letter is sent. A casual reader would never know these two birds had actually met.

In today's organizational white waters, it's harder than ever to find anybody much less someone who might be remotely interested in your product or service. Voice mail, transferred employees, defunct organizations stand in the way. Most folks are too busy with the latest reorganization to get interested in more change. First calls are more difficult, more costly, less productive and more important than ever.

Ground Rules

It's the first meeting. Here we are, just the two of us. Like puppies meeting for the first time, there's a lot of sniffing going on. That's as it should be. This first call is a credential setting meeting for both parties.

The people you meet on first calls want to see if you're "for real." They want to know if you and, by implication, your organization are bright and presentable. (Who knows, they might want to show you off to the boss someday.) Are you worth knowing? Do you have some information they don't have? Are you knowledgeable about their issues, their company, their business? Can you bring something to the party?

At this moment, the person you're meeting with is simply a "contact." You, the seller, want to find out if this person is a prospect, i.e., someone with a problem you can fix and willing to pay money to get it done, or if not, willing to lead you to someone who will. When you first walk into an organization, you're looking for a guide not a buyer. You'll sell one hell of a lot more meetings than product in your career.

Remember, your ultimate objective is to set up that rare moment when a buyer, a seller and the will to act get together in the same room.

No one is going to buy anything at this meeting. That's not its purpose. We've all heard too many "one-call close" stories. These tales are exciting, but upon examination rarely true. Salespeople don't make them up, they just forget the early effort. A heavy-hitter will always tell you how far the ball went, where and when, but you hear little about those long hours of practice. The initial meeting will be frustrating if you go in expecting to hit a home run and make a sale. *Selling product at the first call guarantees a strikeout.*

This first call begins as a ritual exchange. You'll each take a turn at talking as you size each other up, but both parties are not equally committed to making this meeting work. You initiated the call. You are the actor. The other person's in a theatre – front-row center – waiting for the curtain to go up. Here to watch your show. Hopefully, it will be a star turn. But it's up to you to make it enjoyable. And by the way, nobody goes to the theatre to be probed to death with "process" questions.

Our attitude has to be that of the gold miner panning the stream bed. We're going to look at a lot of sand to find a few nuggets. Some miners are better than others; they pan faster or longer. Still others build sluice boxes and sift tons of sand, rather than pounds. The big winners, however, all have a process they follow. A miner who starts panning whenever he sees water doesn't find much gold. The successful miner first looks for evidence. What kind of gravel is in the stream? Where was its source? How fast is the current? Where's the high water line? Then he steps into the river. We can learn from that successful miner. Many of us are doing a lot of panning. *We sell as soon as we see water (a warm body)*. We work too hard. Panning isn't easy, you know. And we don't find as much pay dirt as we ought.

Here is a maxim that will make you rich: *The economic buyer – the person who says, "The problem reports to me" – is never present at the first call.* I know! I know! You can tell me of exceptions, but check your experience. How many times was the buyer at the first meeting? How often have you met a shopper? How often have you made an appointment with a senior manager only to discover that you were meeting instead with a subordinate or a subordinate's subordinate? Organizations designate people to be gatekeepers. Their sole objective is to check you out.

I once made a call on the president of a top-five life insurance company. He was looking for a career program to be offered in several divisions. He liked what he heard, but made it clear I had to sell the division vice presidents. To my surprise, they were the economic buyers.

Whether you agree with my maxim or not, it is always a better tactic to assume the economic buyer is not present at this initial meeting. Following this precept will keep you from selling hard too early in the game. It will force you to talk issues, listen more, and you'll be more likely to get a relationship started. Regardless of who shows up at this first call, your job is not to sell your product, but to gain agreement on the issues it addresses. If, by some chance, the economic buyer really is in the room, nothing is lost by taking an approach that helps prospective buyers to sell themselves on your product.

The first call so far ...

- It's a credential-setting meeting, not a sales event
- The economic buyer is not in the room
- Selling the goat kills the ultimate sale
- It's a search for a prospect

Blind Date

A first call is like a blind date: A lot can go wrong before anything has a chance to go right. Blind dates are notoriously bad ways to start a relationship. There is just so much uncertainty. How should I act? What can or should I say? Who are you? What do you want? What do you *really* want? What should I want or expect?

Some approaches suggest you mirror the other person's behavior. But predicting behavioral styles is like predicting the weather, you're almost always wrong when it matters the most. It takes time to know someone. Forget amateur analysis. Remember your objectives. You scheduled this meeting to:

- Identify a "flesh and blood" problem you can solve
- Start a relationship
- Create some excitement
- Sell a second meeting with more powerful people attending

Then, show up – comfortable, at ease, looking for a chance to have some fun. If you follow my maxim, no one will be asked to buy that damn goat. You will immediately be perceived as more attractive and easy to work with. You're confident enough to ease back. You're planning to learn anything you can. You'll be "listening" to the all the nonverbals. You know how the world works and you're willing to talk about it. You've got stories to tell.

You've made a 30-minute appointment. That time limit was your first promise. Keep it! No matter how ready everybody is to continue, you must say: "This was my promise, I'm prepared to stop now." You'll be surprised how often you are the only one interested in going on. Salespeople think signals of affirmation and understanding mean continue. They don't. Before you know it, your contact is pushing 10 on the MEGO (mine eyes glaze over) index. Don't punish your contact for being accessible.

Be in a hurry to tell your story. Ask crisp questions. Being urgent suggests you've got business and you're a professional. Only bums and surfers have time to spare. Always be the one to end the meeting, even if you only plan to go out to the parking lot and cry. If the contact has to end the meeting, it suggests that you're not sensitive to her, and by inference, not sensitive enough to handle the politics and issues she faces in purchasing your "stuff." If the contact says, "I guess we're finished," she's right – you are.

Maintaining a fast pace for the meeting creates energy. It creates a mood of excitement, expectation, unfinished business. People become more action-oriented and ready to take the next step. Never forget that you're running against the clock. People, priorities, problems are all about to change. *Always be leaving.* Never ask yourself, "How long can I stay?" Ask instead, "How soon can I leave?"

> **The First Call Process**
> 1. Amenities
> 2. The Agenda
> 3. A Turn at Talk
> 4. Sinking the Hook
> 5. The Next Step
> 6. Making it Visible

1. Amenities should be brief. Lengthy, unfocused chit-chat is an impediment to doing business and takes everyone's valuable time.

2. The Agenda

- Who you are
- Who you work for
- Your main business
- A few of your clients
- The time commitment
- Your objective for the meeting

This should take two or three minutes. Be sure to include your *special expertise*. You want to establish your market niche immediately. Always answer the "What makes you different?" question whether it's explicit or not.

The objective should be stated clearly and carefully: "I'm here to tell you a bit about our work and the issues we deal with and to learn more about you and your organization. My purpose is to learn enough to decide if another meeting would be in our mutual interest."

This is your way of signalling in advance that you're not going to inflict the dreaded "close." You'll be amazed to see the other person visibly relax. She can be candid now, can give you positive signals without fear of a premature commitment. We know the economic buyer is not in the room. We know others will need to approve. Why beat this person to death. Give her a break.

People are naturally expressive. Think how much energy you use to keep yourself under control in some emotional situation. If potential prospects believe that "high pressure" is coming down, they defend themselves by carefully controlling their words and their body language. They don't want to give you an opening and, as a result, won't give you any information either.

Think about it. You're here to gather data, create excitement, and maybe gain a potential ally. Backing off pays a huge dividend. Relaxed, the contact is open to real dialogue.

3. A Turn at Talk

Giving your contact a turn at talk gives you a chance to learn if it is truly worth meeting again. Always be willing to defer to the other person and forego your own turn. If this person is willing to talk and respond to your questions, great! You'll find a reason to meet again if only for you to take your turn. Remember, you're building a relationship.

If you do take a turn, talk issues, describe client problems and solutions. Tell stories with lots of picturesque details. Bring little or no goat in view. (By the way, you'll always know when the goat has been on stage, it always brings a price question.)

At your contact's turn, the conversation may go in any direction. So be it. Mediocre salespeople usually put the brain on idle now. The contact's words and actions are background noise. Some salespeople only perk up when they hear a familiar word or two which suggests an issue they can sell against. They often cut the other person off, jump into action, selling hard and self-destructing.

Experts listen acutely to the words, to the silence, to what has not been said. As the contact talks, you need to signal that it has been understood. Use words and gestures like "Yes," "Right!," "Got it," leaning forward, nodding affirmatively (not nodding off). Sales stars always give the speaker a moment or two for additions, amendments, footnotes before responding.

The person you're meeting with has an agenda. You certainly want to know what it is. When people speak there is almost always more than one thing being said. For example: "I claim that 'X' is my most important professional priority." There may be several meta-messages being communicated.

- One, the fact that X is my top priority.
- Two, since I suspect you think X is a big deal, by implication, I merit more respect from you.
- Three, we both know only people of a certain level work on X, so I'm signalling my status.
- Four, I may just be fibbing about X to see your reaction. If you act astonished, that tells me something about how I'm perceived by you.

It would be easy to come up with five, six, seven or a dozen meta-messages from that one statement. Experts use all the tools – experience, intuition, education, brains to sort it out. How something is said is infinitely more important than what is said, and they know it.

4. Sinking the Hook

Selling and fishing have at least this much in common: If you try to sink the hook at the first light nibble on your bait, you won't catch many fish and you will never land a big one. The same is true for a seller who jumps on the first vague, tentative need he hears. Far better, like the expert angler, to put some slack in the line. Ask a few questions:

- Is this need of real concern to the organization?
- Why do you see this as a problem?
- What effects has it had?
- What have you (or your organization) done to fix it?
- Who else cares, really cares?
- Who has the problem, the pain?
- How do they see it?
- What is their understanding of the situation?
- Would anybody spend money on this?
- Has this had other negative effects? (This is a important question. You're fishing for a bigger issue. That other problem might offer an opportunity twice as large as the issue nibbling away now.)

Get enough information so you can *see* the problem. You should have identified the people, e.g., computer programmers, not just "them." You should be able to visualize the problem happening, e.g., complaints to the department head about shift work. You should know if anybody cares. No use proposing a $100 solution for a $10 problem. Don't press too hard; this person probably has few answers. But you do want to determine if the issue is real, not some vague, ethereal need nobody gives a damn about.

Watch for soft "maybe" words like *need, feel, like, want, desire, expect, probably*. They're sure signs that no serious need is in the room. Action language includes words like *commit, stop, achieve, finish, promise, guarantee, complete, avoid, require, demand*. Needs that nobody spends money on always have "always" in the description: "Well, we're always trying to … " or "A good idea is always welcome." Problems that have *always* been around remain that way.

Assuming you've seen a "flesh and blood" issue, you might share an anecdote, a story that adds more urgency to the problem. Try to tell a story with a surprise in it. Every contact is saying, "Tell me something I don't know." If you can, you're well on the way to getting that second meeting. You may be asked to describe how you solve the problem. That's a request for the goat. Show a horn or a hoof. Just enough to suggest that what you have works. Then don't be afraid to ask, "Does this make sense?"

There are only three reasons why contacts agree to another call:

- The Gospel: to learn more about how your product or service will solve their problem.

- Gossip: to gain more information about their business or profession.

- Fun: because they simply expect to enjoy the meeting.

Don't ever tell the whole story. Leave something unanswered. Give the contact a reason to bring you back. As Voltaire said, "The secret of being a bore is to tell everything."

5. The Next Step

Ask about next steps. If the meeting has gone well you might ask: "Assuming for the moment that we have a good solution and the price is right, what is the process for doing business together?" "How do you test an idea like this?"

And always describe your organization's preferred process for making the decision to do business together. Let's say that your closing rate doubles if you get the opportunity to personally present the proposal. If so, now is the time to establish that step. You might say, "Our approach to doing business includes ..." and present the process:

- The initial meeting
- Fact-finding at the plant sites
- A follow-up meeting
- Proposal design
- *My* presentation of the proposal to management
- Management decision on the next step

All too often, salespeople spend energy trying to sell themselves into meetings when they could have established their right to be present simply by stating early in the selling cycle that this is how we mutually decide whether to do business together.

Follow up by detailing your decision procedure in a letter. Make a record of how you want to proceed. Once established, the prospect accepts the sequence as standard. Nothing brings more dismay to a salesperson than a prospect who skips a critical step in the sales cycle or, even worse, decides to handle it herself.

Zig Ziglar, a star salesman and motivational speaker, says that the difference between a professional salesperson and a professional visitor is asking for an order. That's great advice, but an order for what? In this first meeting, your goal is to sell a second meeting. Failing that, you should be selling an idea, a question the contact needs to answer, the seriousness of a problem, even getting another good lead – *anything* but the goat.

Always ask for an action – a quick easy step – and confirm it. Never settle for a hope, ask for a promise. Look for a chance to ask for help. More likely, the contact will want to reflect. That's O.K. Let the "fester factor" go to work. Remember, you'll need at least three interactions to get the relationship in place. This is the time for you to make that little promise – information you'll send, a name, an article, a suggestion for solving a problem discussed during your meeting, etc. Making and keeping little promises makes the prospect more secure and keeps the sales process moving. Make it clear that they will be asked to decide whether or not to meet again. Save your most assertive behavior for later meetings. You can only ask for more after you've made a deposit or two in the prospect's good will account.

No matter where this first meeting ends, respond in writing. If the result was good, describe the next step. If it's over, wish them well, suggest that they call if the situation changes, and tell them you will keep in touch.

6. Making it Visible

You rarely find "love at first sight" at the first call. Most are like a mild, overcast winter day. Not great, not too terrible either. Salespeople going through the motions don't learn a thing or start a relationship. Then they send a perfunctory letter, dictated as they turn in their rental car, as damning proof of their failure. These folks always make a lot of first calls since they rarely get a client to service.

Avoid the kind of dull first-call follow-up displayed in these two examples:

> Dear Paul:
>
> Thanks very much for your time and interest during our meeting December 13th. I appreciated the opportunity to share my story with you, and to learn more about your situation.
>
> Thanks also for your insights and challenging questions during our discussion. They will help us to more effectively position our product. In response to your request for more detailed information on how our system works, I will consult with ____ ____ and respond to you by January 3rd.
>
> Regardless, I'll be in touch in the next couple of weeks to discuss your reaction to our white paper, and to discuss possible next steps in our mutual "discovery process." Thank you again for your time and consideration.
>
> Sincerely,

> Dear Steve:
>
> Thanks very much for your time and continued interest during our meeting December 16th. I wish you the very best for the new year.
>
> As we discussed, we view our system as an enhancement rather than a replacement for existing systems. Should your needs or situation change, or if you're just looking for some fresh ideas, we're at your service.
>
> I'll be inviting you to a "showcase" early in the new year. Again, thank you for your time and consideration. I look forward to future conversations.
>
> Sincerely,

These drab, leaden, lifeless letters are as flat as pavement. The writer is waiting for a happy accident to happen, not trying to create one. This is the work of an amateur hoping to get lucky.

A good follow-up letter:

- Always contains an action step of some kind, be it trivial or grand
- Adds detail to some situation or issue discussed in the meeting
- Is not less intimate than your meeting
- Makes it obvious to a third-party reader that a meeting has occurred. People did actually talk. It was not simply two ships passing in the night
- Should be written so it will make sense to the boss of the person you met – a tough test.

> Dear Elizabeth:
>
> I enjoyed our meeting although it was too short. I felt we had to end it just as we were about to begin. I met with Richard as you suggested and a proposal is in his office now.
>
> You mentioned a woman on the West Coast, someone who is terrific at networking. Clearly, this person is good at relationship building. Running her through basic grade school exercises on relationships would be a waste of time. She can probably teach all of us a thing or two. On the other hand, she may be very weak on cold calling and need some direct, simple steps to follow.
>
> Elizabeth, my point is this: I would much prefer to open any sales training workshop with your folks describing their most difficult sales problems. It will be very clear from this opening exercise what level of training is required. If they need the "basics," they'll get them. If the problem is more subtle, we'll teach it on that level. In effect, build the workshop around known needs rather than prescribing solutions in advance.
>
> I will call Tuesday to learn your decision.
>
> Best regards,

This letter tells a story, brings some new information and positions the product more clearly.

First Call Summary

If you want your first calls to be the start of something more, not the end of something awful, keep in mind:

- The world is complicated. Nobody buys alone.
- The economic buyer is not in the room.
- Your product is your promises. That's what this first contact needs to see most.
- Find an issue you can "see."
- Create a sense of urgency on your part. Always be leaving.
- Send a missive that matters. Write a letter that turns that cloudy winter afternoon into a bright, fresh spring second meeting.

Chapter 7
Marketing to Major Accounts

Two young employees of a major financial services firm installed a 250-million dollar desk-top computer system for their company. They believed the expertise gained from this experience was highly marketable. They quit their jobs on Wall Street and formed a consulting firm.

After the usual struggle to get started, a prospect appeared. Another Wall Street financial service company was changing over to a desk-top system. A 75-million dollar investment. An opportunity!

Their first call was on the coordinator of the project. Frank was a senior manager. His job was to insure a smooth introduction of the new system. They proposed to take a look at it for $60,000. A paltry sum to pay for the experience they had gained installing a quarter-billion dollar system. Frank agreed. However, he couldn't approve the expenditure, only his boss had such authority. "Could we meet with her?" our consultants asked. No, Frank would carry the message. This was bad news. Depending on others to make a sale will soon have you looking for another job.

Contrary to expectations, though, Frank did a good job writing up the idea. His boss, Joan, thought it was a great idea, which Frank reported back to our two consultants. "When can we start?" they queried. "Well, there's a couple of hitches." Huh? "I didn't mention it earlier, but the three line divisions getting the installation are a little unhappy. Oh, they recognize the need, but they had their own alternative. They're not terribly supportive of this corporate effort. I need to do some work to soften them up so they will cooperate with you and that'll take some time. And Joan thought it would be good politics to see if her boss Bruce had any comment on your proposal."

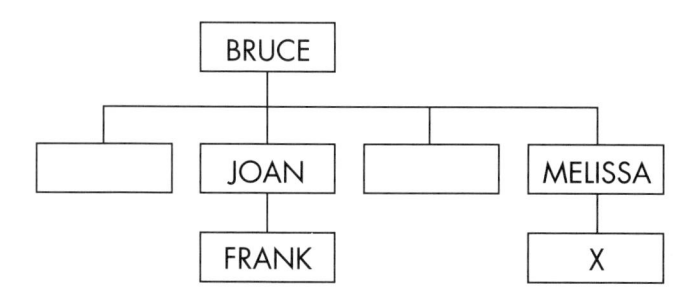

```
                BRUCE
    ┌─────────────┼─────────────┐
    │           JOAN           MELISSA
    │             │             │
    │           FRANK           X
```

Days, weeks pass. Calls, letters go to and from Frank and our consultants. Finally a strategy meeting is scheduled. Frank opens with news. His boss's boss Bruce had circulated the proposal to his other direct reports for comment. The good news: They had all commented favorably. The bad news: One of Bruce's reports, Melissa, had instructed one of her subordinates to work with Frank to see if any other consulting firms should also be considered. Frank is chagrined.

It looks now like he will have to seek out other consultants so he can be politically safe. Do they know of anybody he could talk to?!!!

Sound familiar? It should. This scenario is becoming more and more common. In today's corporation, it's rare that only one person is responsible for a decision. The smallest sale requires multiple approvals every step of the way. We've had our information revolution and now businesses are drowning in data. Every idea can and usually is revisited over and over again. Someone always suggests one more variable (computers create new variables at an astounding rate) to study before commitment. The result is delay and apathy.

Growing complexity and growing competition have complicated the decision-making process even further. The need to respond quickly becomes more vital to success. More and more systems are installed. Reorganizations, mergers, acquisitions, downsizing are further attempts to streamline operations. Paradoxically, the net effect is an even slower response time. Who's responsible for what becomes vague and uncertain. This is truly how the world works in business-to-business sales of systems and service. Many sales theories begin with the economic buyer, the seller and the will to act on the same room. In fact, that's the end of the modern sales cycle. Ninety-five percent of a salesperson's time is spent to create that moment.

That experience of our two young computer consultants makes a dreary tale. Here are some ideas to ward off that sad result in your sales career.

Who is the Buyer?

In a big-ticket business-to-business sale, lots of people have to be sold who can't buy anything. They need to "buy in." One sure way to protect yourself from selling too soon is to assume that economic buyers never show up at the first call. If by some rare chance they are present, let them prove it! By the way, was Frank the economic buyer in our story? If not, who was?

Here's another story: Kathy, my Southern sales representative, got a lead from a trade convention. A phone call to the lead, Bob, brought this data: He loved our stuff. He had heard nothing but great things. Could they get together in Birmingham? Sure! was Kathy's response. At that meeting, Kathy recommended that Bob attend an upcoming showcase. Bob thought that was a great idea and suggested that he would bring his boss and two other interested vice presidents, one from Acquisitions, the other from Planning.

The day of the showcase arrived. Bob couldn't make it, but the three vice presidents did. They were impressed. "We need this. How can we get started? We'd like to go ahead." Kathy immediately put together a proposal and sent it to Bob's boss. A done deal, as they say, but no response was forthcoming. Kathy called. A secretary called back. "Sorry, we have decided not to proceed." Her calls to the other vice presidents were not returned. Finally, she called Bob. "What's happened?" "Oh, my boss got a little carried away," he replied. "It's just out of the question. I can't run your program without help, so I told them late next year at the earliest." !!!

Here's a guy who brought us in, then kicked us out. He didn't have the money or the pain, but his approval was critical. Kathy assumed this guy was a green light. He was, but he wanted to be consulted every step of the way. In addition, he had another objective. He wanted to leverage the purchase into some empire building for himself – another associate reporting to him.

Ya gotta talk. Ya gotta meet. Ya gotta listen to all the players. Nobody likes being taken for granted.

Remember Frank in our opening story? He wanted the deal to go through, but he tried to carry the ball alone. Any time spent on what Frank wanted for Frank out of the deal would have been a wise investment. Our guys would have uncovered more of the political picture. And the more personal gain Frank saw in the proposal, the more likely he would have involved them in helping him sell the project. A prospect becomes your champion as his personal gain from doing business with you increases.

Every top salesperson makes it a point to find out what's in it for the prospect and approvers. That's the key to finding the potential problems standing in the way of getting the deal. Generally, one player gains face at the expense of another or at least most people perceive the situation that way. Remember, buyers have rivals. You have to find the "losers" in your transaction and find enough payoff for them to go along. "What's in it for me?" is a question that requires a positive answer for all the key players.

Our two computer consultants should have been selling meetings not the product. "Who else should hear our story?" should have been their first priority. *Nobody buys alone, nobody!* If they truly understood that, they would have pushed hard to meet others. Had they met one other person, it's likely that important sales data would have emerged – other players, other issues.

They detailed their services too soon. If we know that others must buy in, we also know we will probably have to modify our proposal to meet their needs. Too much goat locks people out and gives them something to shoot at before the complete alternative is even on the table.

One Niche at a Time

"But if I don't talk much goat, what will I emphasize when it's my turn at talk?" That's easy. Answer the most important question the prospect has and for which salespeople usually give the poorest answer: "Why should I push for or choose you?"

There's competition aplenty everywhere you look. Take a product like disposable diapers. In 1991, over 69 new sizes and types were introduced in that market segment alone. Competition is like dandelions. It spreads with the wind, seems to be everywhere and is damn near impossible to get rid of. What does make you and your services special? How do you differentiate yourself from your competition?

You can't simply sell features, advantages and benefits in the face of fierce competition. Your message will sound like everyone else's. That won't get your prospect out of his chair or get his heart beating faster. It's too bland, too mushy, too weak, too much the "same old stuff." Soon you're out the door and out of mind.

A friend of mine, a chief financial officer, for a small business had just been fired. He was caught in a merger. The market was glutted. One local advertisement for a CFO had garnered over 500 resumes. He had impeccable credentials. So did the competition. He was depressed. Interviews were not going well. He talked his capabilities, his strengths, his experience, to no avail. Others had more or better. I asked him, "What's unique or different about your experience compared to the other 499?" As he answered that question, his eyes lit up, he became animated and proud. He spoke about how unusual it was for a CPA to be with a company that started without a nickel in the till and became a multi-million dollar business. He had wonderful war stories about that experience. I told him to talk about that "stuff," somebody will buy, and they did. It made him one of a kind. It made him a star. Talking differences can do the same for you. They affirmatively answer the prospect's question: "What makes you special?"

Making a Difference

Being a good salesperson is not enough today, you must also be a marketing expert. A marketer talks "differences" – what it is that makes you and your stuff uniquely set apart from the competition, from traditional approaches, from the market place, the rest of the world. Many salespeople can't market. When faced with the prospect question, "How are you better?," they knock the competition or restate product features. They're much like the late Gilda Radner on Saturday Night Live, who did the news for the deaf by simply shouting the stories. Every "how better?" question should get a "how we're different" answer. This distinction is not some small semantic quibble. Claims of "better" or "more" are discounted as mere assertions. Differences are seen as facts.

Most of the people you see are feasibility buyers of one kind or another. They can't authorize the money, but they need to approve. They're not feeling the pain, so they feel less urgency to act. They ask to see the goat and then are bored with the details.

Selling people a product they don't especially need is not much fun for anyone. No matter what questions they officially put on the table, their true question is: Can you tell me something I don't know or alert me to something I should care about?

Talking differences is safer than talking product in those early calls. For one thing, it is new information. It helps the various buyers position your product and services without deadening product detail. It makes them more effective in communicating what you do to others. Selling "differences" makes you unique, special. Creating that niche protects you from price competition. It eliminates the "apples to apples" comparisons which ultimately come down to price only. You will never have enough product advantages to overwhelm half-price competition. Only differences provide the "added value."

To identify differences you always need to phrase the question: "What's different about ... compared to ... ?" There has to be a comparison. Without that contrast, it's like asking the question, "What's different about a duck?" with no other fowl in sight.

Most folks start with their product or service and ask themselves what's different from the competitor's. Well, those are differences all right, but in a competitive world, they're not enough. To do the job right, you need more than the goat. Look at your company's philosophy. How is it different from others? How is your organization's approach to solving problems uniquely suited to the world we live in? The most powerful differences are philosophical – your view of how the world works or doesn't work. Talking about your "philosophy" gets you excited and enthusiasm is a communicable disease.

What is unique about your delivery, installation, maintenance, follow-up compared to others? What about your colleagues? What do they bring to the party that's unparalleled in your field? What about your company's values? What does your company stand for? Johnson & Johnson's commitment to their credo – a published set of ethics – has made them one of the most admired companies in the world and carried them through critical marketing crises like the Tylenol scare. What about YOU? You are, in fact, the biggest difference from the competition. Remember, your promises are most of what the customer is buying.

If you want to stand out from your competition, write out three or four differences, not related to your product, and talk about them on your next sales call. Watch the temperature rise in the meeting room.

In summary:

- "Who else should know?" is your top priority.
- Sell meetings. Nobody buys alone.
- Talk differences. Establish your uniqueness early and often.
- Keep the complete "goat" off the table as long as possible. You need space and time to fold in everyone's agenda.
- Never, never let somebody else sell for you.

ILLINOIS BELL – A CASE STUDY

What follows is a memo written at my request by my top salesman. I had asked him to tell how he landed the largest account Blessing/White had gotten in ten years. It demonstrates the diligent, often indirect, approach required in marketing to major accounts. Individual names have been changed, but not the client, nor the salesman, nor his story.

> *The history of Illinois Bell actually goes back to the mid-1970's. One of the first instructors I ever trained was Elizabeth, then at Continental Bank. She delivered programs for about a year at Continental Bank and then left the organization. She wound up at Illinois Bell.*
>
> *As I do with any instructor that I can track, I kept in touch with Betty, calling her two or three times a year, making it a point to take her to lunch at least once a year. It was during one of these lunches in 1983 that she said, "You know, you ought to be talking to Carol in the Career Development department – they're getting ready to do something." That statement was well worth all these lunches.*
>
> *I called Carol, whose name I would not have gotten in almost any other way. Carol is a relatively anonymous person even inside the organization and would have been hard to find. She agreed to a meeting. I'm rarely late for meetings, but I was a good 30 minutes late for this one. As a result, I only had about 30 minutes to talk with Carol and her assistant, Mary Ellen. By the time we got done with the introductions and the small talk, I was down to about 20 minutes. I must have covered a lot of ground in a hurry. Nevertheless, something*

I said must have struck a nerve, because about a month later they called me to come back and talk some more, albeit more slowly.

Carol had two interns working on their "career" project. They were pretty well down the line with their design. In fact, they had been to another Bell company and come away with a vague copy of what was then that organization's career "system" – a typically soft, rambling, patchwork collection of instruments, job matching techniques, counselling interventions and so forth. At this second meeting, they asked me to comment on what Blessing/White did to improve the coaching/counselling techniques of managers. That was their specific interest at the outset.

Before answering, I asked them to tell me what they were doing and why they were doing it. They laid out their objectives, which were remarkably similar to our Basic Beliefs. They also presented the entire borrowed Indiana Bell approach. I didn't say it wouldn't work. I said that we had virtually the same objectives but that we went about it differently. I also told them that we didn't do much to improve the coaching/counselling skills of managers and that we couldn't help them in that regard, that we didn't think that 'counselling' was the way to go. I didn't say much more.

Naturally they wanted to know much more about what we did do. With their objectives as a lead-in (virtually identical to our objectives, as I said above), I was able to do a presentation on how we approached the issue.

My audience at this point consisted of the two interns and Mary Ellen.

It was an interesting experience. Their eyes literally grew wider and wider. At this point I introduced the profiling techniques and instruments for the first time. They could barely contain themselves.

From that point on, it was just a matter of time. The next meeting was with Carol, Mary Ellen, the interns and Carol's boss (Bob). At that meeting we got a general agreement that our approach was worth looking into further and specific agreement to go to a pilot program. One of Carol's great talents is to make things happen. She had it set up in fairly short order. I taught the pilot. They paid for it. I did an evaluation, it was a success.

The next step was to meet again with Carol's boss (Bob) and with a very influential person where the decision was concerned, Harriet. Harriet had been at Illinois Bell damn near forever. Her retirement was imminent (within the coming year). Harriet had an awful lot of presence and an awful lot of clout. We were clearly being vetted by Harriet. One issue was any overt or latent sexism attendant to the program or the purveyor (us). We got Harriet's approval. It was critical. If we had not it would have been over right then and there. Harriet has long since retired. I continue to invite Harriet to Blessing/White's Christmas Party. She'll get invited as long as I'm issuing invitations.

Our next meeting was with Carol, Mary Ellen, Bob, Harriet, the interns, and a few other people who are involved. At this point, we decided (they decided) to customize the package. Their reason was that they wanted to present something that was Illinois Bell-specific, and new... they wanted to be very sure that people didn't see this as the same old stuff being rolled out by Corporate or another vestige of the old Bell system thinking. They quickly hit upon the customized "You, Inc." concept.

We still had to go on and get many higher level approvals for all of this. Carol's boss' boss, Bailey (a fourth level) was the next important hurdle. Bailey is a bright, intelligent (and truly intellectual) guy who knows how to make things happen inside the Illinois Bell organization. Very respected, very influential. Carol had him pretty much on board by the time we came back for the next session. That was a formal presentation to Bailey's boss and others at his level in the organization. Virtually the entire HR staff was there, along with people from Public Relations, a couple of key departments, some people from an ineffectual but influential career "task force" (who had to be convinced without having their toes stepped on), and a pretty wide-spread cast of characters. This was an intensely political meeting.

At this point, Carol and I began doing co-presentations. She would present the issues. Chief among her data were the findings from their Work Relationships Survey. Invariably, the Work Relationships Surveys turn up bitching about careers, advancement, about help and support from the boss, etc. They do them annually in some companies, giving them base-lines, national norms and trends.

Selling The Big Ticket 111

Carol would lay this stuff on chapter and verse, and then I would come on up and do a presentation. The MPG presentation depended heavily upon demographic trends in the world outside, (i.e., plateauing, baby booming, the elimination of middle management jobs, etc.).

When we got the go-ahead from these people we were almost home free but there were several other meetings we had to do. Carol and I again teamed up and did joint presentations for several selected key line managers and their staffs. We also did one for the president's staff, although the president wasn't on hand.

The feedback was positive on all the meetings. There were virtually no problems. We submitted a proposal. It was a one-page proposal outlining two fairly simple alternatives. They responded by giving us the go-ahead and sending us the check four months in advance of the delivery of the customized materials.

Following the go-ahead and the mailing of the invoice there was yet much work to do. We had agreed that we would do a series of very high-level management education meetings. Carol and I then did three large group meetings for the fourth, fifth, and sixth level managers. Every one of them attended one session or another. Bailey, Carol and I gave them a formal three-hour presentation with slides, bells, whistles, video-tape, etc.

The next step was to set up and conduct an in-house train the trainer. Carol did not have indigenous staff to work with. We/she had to solicit volunteers from first-level management positions throughout the organization. These people did not come from the training department. They had to be recruited, wooed, and trained. We got quite a collection. We had some very good candidates and we had some real lulus. They almost all wound up teaching programs. Some did a lot better than others, but even the worst managed to get the job done.

The summary of the key elements of Illinois Bell would include the following:

- *Follow up on all [contacts]. Never lose track of them. Sooner or later one of them will say "You ought to be talking to so and so ..."*

- *Our entry to Illinois Bell began with the lowest of the low. The first real converts we had were the two interns. These weren't even permanent staff employees. (Both have gone on to become full-time employees. One has moved to the Network Operations department, and all by herself now constitutes a second major buying point. She is now buying MPG Support Staff for Network Operations. The first order was $70,000 worth.)*

- *Staff people know their organizations and will help you move upward and sell upward in the organization. Listen carefully to them.*

- *In organizations like these, no assumptions about who's important and who isn't can be made. Without question, Harriet could have stopped the whole shootin' match in mid-stream. She wasn't even in the buying chain of command.*

- *You can't make too many presentations. The more they want the more likely you are to succeed. Each presentation is not another hurdle to be overcome – it's another collection of allies and supporters to put in your pocket.*

- *The amount of client service you must provide during the early stages of the sale and the early implementation stages is critical. Above I've only mentioned the number of formal presentations I've made. I can not tell you how many meetings I had with Carol, with Mary Ellen, with the interns, to plan things, to write brochures, to suggest strategies, to educate people, and so on.*

That memo illustrates the critical points in making a multiple-approval sale, as well as the incredible perseverance of a great salesman – Neil Thompson.

Chapter 8
The Second Time Around – Act I

"Love is lovelier, the second time around." So goes the old popular song. Believe it or not, the second meeting on an account is just as wonderful. Somebody might show up with real trouble. Of course, there's no guarantee that live interest will be in attendance. You might not see your dream date until three, four, who knows how many more meetings.

When you've got lots of approvers, you can be sure whatever you're proposing is a big deal to somebody. So everything is a big deal nowadays and big deals take time.

What's there to do "till love comes 'round"? Plenty! You need to qualify the account. You're looking for answers to these questions:

- Do the prospective buyers really need my product?

- Do the folks at the top agree? If not, will I get a chance to tell my story to them?
- Will I be able to identify all the players – approvers, blockers, deal breakers, naysayers, buyers – affecting the buying decision?
- Can I make a good case for my product or service as an answer?
- Do I have a champion?

Obviously, you need a yes to all these questions. That takes time and meetings. When purchasing agents were asked to name the typical shortcoming among salespeople who call on their companies, the most common response was failure to call on enough people in the customer's organization.

At the first call, you sent up a few trial balloons – issues, problems, opportunities. One of those connected and this second meeting was the result. At this meeting *and every subsequent meeting,* you should follow the same process. Whether it's a casual one with your champion over lunch or the final formal presentation, the approach you need to take remains the same. Depending on the circumstances, you may cover only part of the process. If that is the case, go over the earlier steps at your next meeting before proceeding.

Every meeting is unique. We always know "Unexpected" will be attending. Maybe even "Gotcha" will come. Nevertheless, I've found this sequence most useful in meeting the different needs of the seller and the buyer. Start with this "program" and let events get in the way.

PLAYBILL

The Second Time Around in Three Acts

Prologue

Act One

Scene One .... The Positioning Statement
Scene Two .... The Situation as I Understand It

Act Two

Scene One .... Setting the Stage for the Solution
Scene Two .... Selling Differences
Scene Three ...... A Hoof, A Horn

Act Three

Scene One .... Action Steps
Scene Two .... Dealing with Concerns

Prologue

This meeting was scheduled because someone in this account is interested, maybe even excited, about your stuff. He or she sees it as a possible solution to a personal issue *and* an organizational need. There's a prospect here tonight!

Never forget that the person who scheduled this meeting has some personal risk. He could lose face if you fall on yours. Often this person has been given responsibility to find a solution to the problem under discussion. In fact, he may have been expressly hired to do what you're selling. By the second meeting, you need to have thought through how to help this person save or maintain face and buy your solution. Many a sale has sunk on this reef. This person needs to know "Are you my ally or my enemy?"

Often this person will become your champion. After all, he's the one who found you. Everybody loves their own baby. By the way, some folks confuse a mentor and a champion. A mentor is someone who gives you advice. You don't need advice here, you need action. A champion is a militant advocate for you. He's pushing you and your service.

A champion is the key to the major-account sale. Without one, you'll never identify all the players in your particular game. He or she provides the internal support and energy you must have to move the bureaucracy off dead center. You need help to get your wagon rolling.

Take care of your champions. Always tell them something no one else in the account knows – a price discount, additional research, other supporting evidence, client testimonials, etc. Your job is to increase their organizational net worth. You want to make them "look smart."

Anytime you spend taking a champion "back stage" is worth it. Tell her about your company, colleagues, business practices, everything. Bring her "inside" your organization. Never miss a chance to quietly affirm what each of you has to gain from this relationship. Think of your champions as your business partners!

If the meeting is going to have some heavy hitters in it, do everything you can to talk or meet with them in advance.

- How do they view the issue?
- What do they want to accomplish at the meeting?
- What do they see as possible outcomes?
- Who do they rely on for advice?

Never walk into a meeting without knowing what will make the big guns fire, or their direction. No professional sports team goes into a game without a scouting report. Neither should you.

Don't let this happen to you: It was the big day. Finally a meeting with a mover and shaker, a driver-driver, a master of the universe; somebody who could spend big money and did. The vice president marched into the room with a lieutenant, or was it a private? Introductions were perfunctory, "This is one of our analysts, Tony Z..." The last name was lost as the pair settled in. The salesman made a great presentation. He focused all his attention and energy on El Supremo. It was time to ask about next steps and our fellow did. Surprisingly, the vice president turned to Tony for an opinion, actually for the decision. And what did Tony do? He said, "Forget it." Thanks but no thanks.

When you make your presentations, never make assumptions about who counts. Always sell to everyone in the room, not just the Big Boss. Don't cause others to lose face through your inattention.

Act One

Scene One: The Positioning Statement

After the first meeting, the concern of the prospects changes. You've got their interest – a bit – and they've seen something in you – who knows what? – that they like. Now their question is: "Yeah, I think I've got that problem and, besides that, I've got 20 guys knocking on my door saying they can fix it. What makes you special?"

As this meeting gets underway, always assume you're a stranger. Never expect anyone to remember. Tell who you are. Describe your company and what your business is. State the general purpose of or decision to be made at this meeting. Don't assume everybody knows why they're in the room; they don't. In my own experience, warm bodies are occasionally dragooned simply to fill the chairs.

If you have identified some strategic, philosophical differences from your competition, mention them now. Some salespeople talk through the meeting objectives at this time. That's a bad idea. Nobody much cares at this point and the energy level in the room will drop. Better to get down to the issue and use the objectives later to summarize the meeting. They carry a lot more meaning after the context and problem have been established.

Scene Two: The Situation As I Understand It

You're meeting because a flesh and blood issue has surfaced. Now you need to work it through. Getting a deeper understanding of and agreement on "the issue" produces excitement and provides the impetus for the group to make something happen.

After your introductory remarks, you begin with these words or something similar: "The situation as I understand it is as follows... ." This is a pointed statement of the problem, its suspected cause or causes and the direction that needs to be taken if it is to be solved. You also cast gloom around by predicting dire consequences if no change is made. You then ask, "Is this correct?" FULL STOP. Wait for a response. Ask individuals by name if necessary. If you get agreement, ask what else can be added to the group's understanding. If there is dissent, fine. Be the moderator. Get all the details you can. An archaeologist looks at pottery shards and constructs a civilization, you're piecing together a clear picture of the issue from shards of information. Let people talk.

This is the critical step. Why would anybody buy if they're not sure what would be fixed or better as a result? This step could eat up all your presentation time. If so, let it be. Schedule another meeting. You can bet that each attendee has a different position, based upon different assumptions about what the real world is like. So you have to start out by establishing what is real. This is the situation as you understand it. You fold in any new information like adding beaten egg whites to a waffle mix.

You must get agreement on what's going on, on how the world is working right now in this organization. The deeper the agreement – "That's right!"; "Amen, Brother!" – the more likely your product or service will be perceived as an effective response to the issues and problems that world presents.

At this point you need commitment, conviction from the group. At least some of them should sit up, their pulses quickening, and say, "Yes, that's it! Those are our real problems!" If the economic buyer is in the room, he or she must be on board at this point. You've pointed out some problems more clearly and forcefully than they've been articulated before. If most of the group scratches and remains unimpressed, all the rest of your work will be in vain. Getting belief in your presentation of the situation and its main problems is so important that you don't proceed until you *know* you have significant agreement.

Your restatement of the situation establishes your credentials. You just helped your prospects take a giant step toward clarity and agreement about the problem. It's been established that there's trouble in River City. As scientist Charles Kettering said: "A problem well stated is half solved." To that I would add "and the sale is 90% made."

PLAYBILL

The Second Time Around in Three Acts

Prologue

Act One

Scene One ....The Positioning Statement
Scene Two ....The Situation as I Understand It

Act Two

Scene One ....Setting the Stage for the Solution
Scene Two ....Selling Differences
Scene Three ......A Hoof, A Horn

Act Three

Scene One ....Action Steps
Scene Two ....Dealing with Concerns

Chapter 9

The Second Time Around – Act II

"Love is lovelier, the second time around, just as wonderful with both feet on the ground." Act II has both feet on the ground. It promises a practical, workable remedy. Amateur salespeople trot out the goat, laying on detail after detail about their product or service, and hope the audience sees the connection between the question raised in Act I and the answer (Act II). The connection may be obvious to those of us in the know, but the poor prospect is more likely than not to be perplexed. "What is that goat doing here?" Or to bring the analogy closer to home: "Whaddaya mean... voice mail, a training program, a distribution center... will solve our problem?" You haven't begun to tell them about your goat and you have the sinking feeling that they may not like any kind of goat, period!!!

Act Two

Scene One: Setting the Stage for the Solution

Let's slow down a bit. Your audience wants the answer to two questions in Act II – "Can you do it (solve my problem)?" and "Do we want to work with you?" You're not going to get this sale strictly on the technical capabilities of your product or service. Your organization's expertise may have gotten you into the final set. Now all your competition looks equally strong on the product side of the purchase.

Out beyond the footlights, the audience is taking a long look at you and your promises. You are the focus of their attention. The goat is of secondary interest.

Some of your promises were:

- I clearly understand your problem
- I have a simple solution
- I am an expert in my field
- I will make you look good
- I can be trusted

And the most important promise of all: *I am the person responsible for the results promised to you.* Always bring the gospel – the good news that the problem can be solved easily and you will handle all the details. This is a key statement. Every major account buyer knows that she or he is buying a relationship as well as a product.

The data your audience will use to decide if you keep your promises will be intuitive and based on impressions. Every sale is an emotional event as well as a logical decision.

You will need to appeal to the heart and the head. If you ever planned to "show up" at this account, now is the time.

Scene Two: Selling Differences

Always start your solution by talking about differences. Differences in philosophy, differences in handling the problem, differences from your competition (I always labeled the competition as traditional, as in "Our approach differs from traditional approaches in these ways ..."), differences in methodology, differences regarding service, maintenance, implementation. Obviously, you're going to choose differences that you believe will appeal to the prospect. Make your list of three or four differences visible on an easel or blackboard. Don't just let them float out into the ether. Nail them down.

Never forget that you are trying to establish that you, your organization, your product or your service are unique. There is a lot of competition out there. On the surface, it looks just like you and some of it is cheaper. You must add value to your product. Again, its marketing first – creating your niche or position – then selling.

Scene Three: A Hoof, A Horn

As you discuss a difference, the prospect will likely agree – "Hey, that's important"; "That's our view"; "Sounds great, but how do you accomplish it?" Whether you're selling a discrete product, a service or a system, they want some details – the goat. *Now is the time.* Showing a part of the goat to further explain a difference is marketing at its best. You've created a gorgeous mountain range with your definition of the issue and your differences. The prospect can see a cliff edge that needs a goat standing on it to complete the picture. Within that context, your product is seen as a unique solution.

Obviously Act II will not roll out in a straight line. You might mention a difference – "All our systems fail safe"; "Top management must be involved in every installation"; "Our approach is based on self-management," etc. A prospect might go in any number of directions: "Is it really a difference?"; "Why do you believe that?"; "How do you do it?"; "Tell me more." Your response could be a hoof, a horn, a story of client use or results, more background on your organization's philosophy. Whatever your choice, by starting with differences, you've created the context to make you distinct.

Keep the discussion focused around the single issue you are developing. As a kid growing up in the Midwest, I used to fish in a pay lake. Now, a pay lake was usually an artificially-created, mud-bottomed pond periodically stocked with fish – mostly catfish. Old-timers would come to the lake, pay two bucks, and unfurl six or seven fishing rods. These were huge poles, each equipped with heavy duty line, three or four hooks, and a large lead weight at the line's end.

Soon seven lines would be in the water. It was quite a sight. Our fisherman would hear the line being pulled off a reel by a fish. By the time he yanked the right pole, the fish and bait would be gone, and usually the next half hour would be spent untangling lines after his feverish flurry of activity.

Some salespeople are like those old-timers. At this juncture in the meeting, they have everybody's attention so they relax and begin to mix messages and send too many. Boy, do their lines get tangled! Never forget that a specific issue has been identified; the buyers are examining your answer. Always clarity, clarity! Keep your responses simple and on the point. The buyer always wants more certainty.

Bluebirds

The meeting's going well. You're on track and in tune. The signals are positive. They like your stuff and are letting you know it. There's just one more little fact, one more benefit, one more advantage you could tell them. It would be the coup de grace, the final, unexpected twist. So you share it. Looks of expectation turn to bewilderment. Oh, it does *that* too. You see, literally see, your sale fluttering away.

Yep, you did it! You added that last little bluebird to your painting. That little extra touch they didn't ask for and you thought they would love. Never, never throw in one more feature or benefit as an added plus. The buyer has a problem, tell him how to solve it. Don't tell him about the additional capabilities which fix other problems.

The 18th-century Italian painter Canaletto sold hundreds of Venetian landscapes to every Englishman who could afford one. After they bought, he never painted one or two bluebirds in the corner for good measure. Follow his example.

Shortly after forming our company, Tod White – my friend and partner at Blessing/White – and I made several calls on the Prudential Life Insurance Company in Newark, New Jersey. Over the course of several meetings, various middle managers had described their requirements for a career planning seminar. Our design was enthusiastically accepted by all concerned. We had a "done deal," as they say. All that remained was a pro forma meeting with a very senior executive responsible for the project.

It was an informal meeting. We sat on a couch chatting and finishing coffee. The executive noted how positive the comments had been on our work to date. He asked about our philosophical approach. We both jumped in with gusto. I tramped on Tod's words and he "improved" my sentences. One thing led to another and pretty soon Tod and I were discussing other ways to solve this problem at Prudential. We also had a few minor disagreements.

Twenty-five minutes later we were gently, quietly eased out the door with a "We'll get back to you in a few days." Well they did. We were dead. This incident occurred twenty years ago and it still seems like yesterday. We learned a lot from that meeting. For one thing, Tod and I never made a call together again. We had plenty of synergy, but in front of a client, it came across as confusion and conflict. And nobody is buying much of that.

Remember that you are expected to introduce more certainty and clarity into this ambiguous world. Keep your discussion focused on a clear and specific solution to your prospect's problem. And when they've bought that solution, don't embellish or second-guess your own success!

Selling it Right

Most salespeople believe fervently in their product and they see it getting results for their clients. That's great, but some of them go overboard. They decide that if a client's going to buy, they're going to buy it "right." You may only want to buy a cheap fax machine, but you're gonna be "trained" first – "You're really gonna understand what this baby can do. I'll personally come back next week to show you. Boy, we're gonna do it right." And you might just say, "Forget it, I only wanted a fax."

Selling it right is a recurring infection, like malaria, with sellers of services. When the disease is raging, it's almost impossible to buy from these folks because of the added bells and whistles, analyses, gingerbread. You can hardly see the tree for the ornaments. Be on your guard against this disease.

Do not expect every client to adopt the ideal solution to every problem. Many clients will buy into a lesser solution, short of state-of-the art, but workable for them. Don't forget that you're trying to increase your buyer's net worth by solving this problem. You want her to save time, look good, etc. You're selling "making it easy" not "work harder."

At the End of Act II

Throughout the meeting, be willing to let your audience talk. They can't say yes if they're not permitted to speak. When people start talking, they start to think, and the energy level comes up.

If this was an early discovery meeting with a major account, we should not have told our complete story. If one issue was clarified, one difference shown to be a difference that mattered, we're making progress. If this was a major meeting – economic buyer(s) in the room, a decision possible – our presentation will be more comprehensive, but still focused on the main issue (no bluebirds). Act II always starts with differences and, hopefully, ends with an answer that makes sense to the audience.

PLAYBILL

The Second Time Around in Three Acts

Prologue

Act One

Scene One .... The Positioning Statement
Scene Two .... The Situation as I Understand It

Act Two

Scene One .... Setting the Stage for the Solution
Scene Two .... Selling Differences
Scene Three ...... A Hoof, A Horn

Act Three

Scene One .... Action Steps
Scene Two .... Dealing with Concerns

Chapter 10

The Second Time Around – Act III

"Love is lovelier, the second time around, just as wonderful with both feet on the ground. It's that second time you hear your love song sung... ." We know the song we love to hear – an order for business! Ah, sweet, sweet music. If most of your audience liked the first two acts, the third in our drama is anticlimactic. It's a conversation about implementation, getting started, and barriers to action. The commitment has been made, the question is "How?"

Act Three

Scene One: Action Steps

Act III opens with you asking: "Assuming I've answered your immediate questions, is it appropriate to discuss the next step?" This question is directed to the economic buyer. An affirming nod, a glance, an agreeable look is the signal to continue.

Sometimes a quirky sales ego demands more than a quiet yes. The ego wants the buyer to prove how much they want the service or product. They force the buyer to say, "I want it now." Acquiescence isn't enough; they want an energetic, positive "yes." That's too much to ask.

Often, people will buy, but they don't want to be seen as overenthusiastic. They love it, but things can go wrong. Often, a yes of real agreement is never spoken. A lower profile might make more sense politically. A public "yes" can be seen as a sign of weakness. Closing hard can close the door in a hurry. In life, great love affairs have begun with a nod rather than a resounding "yes." Business works the same way.

Once you see or hear a yes, outline the next steps. Make these visible on a flip chart, blackboard or poster. Visibility makes choices conscious. The group learns what its responsibilities are. There are four actions the group can take:

- Buy it
- Try it (a test, trial period, experiment, look-see)
- Tell others (more "second" meetings)
- Do nothing

Obviously, you want them to buy it. It's not bad manners to tell people, "We want your business" and ask, "Is there any reason we can't go forward?" Now is the time to use your most powerful closing technique – a long pause. Give the group a chance to come to a consensus.

When you get the yes that means you've got the sale, the economic buyer only has one question – How do we get started? "I'll handle the details" is your response and promise. Occasionally some non-economic approver will want to reopen some topic or talk more goat. Don't do it. Say you'll meet later ... anything. Tell the buyer everything will be confirmed in writing and on her desk tomorrow. Get out of there, set a date to meet with your champion and celebrate!

Scene Two: Dealing with Concerns

What if you can't move forward because you don't yet have that affirmative response you're hoping for? Your intuition has a big role to play here. If you *know* objections or concerns are likely to be raised, don't wait for proof by inviting them; present them yourself first. Show that you're on top of the situation, not surprised by it.

Frequently you'll get a "not yet." Frankly, I don't like a quick yes. We live in a society where yes doesn't necessarily mean "let's do it!" It can mean "go on," "continue," or it may merely be a social convention to acknowledge, "Yes, I know you're talking."

A few "not yets" help us uncover concerns and potential problems. They give us the opportunity to detail implementation, and to show a bit more of the goat. We can demonstrate more of our expertise and our professionalism. "Not yets" can be our friends. They are signals of interest. They cement the sale. Old-fashioned sales techniques were designed to keep the prospect from saying "not yet" or "no." They figured if you kept the prospects saying "yes," they would finally agree to buy something. In fact, this approach only annoys the prospect and loses sales.

If you get a question you can't handle, say so. Explain your plan to get the answer. If the question is big enough, the meeting might be recessed or adjourned. Why not? This isn't the 1890s; you'll be back in town again. This isn't the only stop you plan to make at this company. Hopefully, this is simply the start of something big. You're building a relationship here as well as making a sale.

All meetings should end with some commitment to action. The prospective buyers may not have bought your complete proposal, but rather chose a test or another meeting. That's a good result. They're sold, but they need to sell others. A big deal needs to simmer. Turn on the heat and you may just burn your commission. Always confirm the commitment, whatever it is, in writing. If the prospect just wants to think it over, ask "Who should I call to learn of your decision and when?"

Claims and Proof

Occasionally someone will ask for proof of your claims. They have every right to do so. People have fears: "Is it really as good as it looks?" "My boss, peers, won't like it." "Are the results over-blown?" Lots of sales are lost here. The buyer has agreed with your assessment, your approach, your answer and she wants a bit of proof for reassurance. Who can blame her. This is big trouble and probably big money.

Salespeople often respond with more claims. They talk about how their product or service will do the job. The buyer is still anxious. At this point most salespeople continue talking, making more reassuring noises. Look, talk is not proof! Trying to supply proof with your own words is a major cause of blown sales calls. A proof is sighted, not cited! The writer Gracian said 500 years ago, "The truth is generally seen, rarely heard."

Proof is a document. At the minimum, it's a third-party statement recounted by you. You should have a proof for every claim you make. Always carry at least one proof document with you at all times. Photographs – of the people making the testimonials, the system at work, et al. – are especially powerful. When asked for proof, show it and shut up. If you get a follow-up question, defer it, if possible, to after the meeting. That question probably came from a feasibility buyer who has many other follow-up questions besides the one on the table. Responding in detail here disrupts the rhythm of the meeting.

You have to listen carefully for a call for proof. Rarely does a prospect say, "Prove it." They usually ask "how" questions. "How does it really work?" is usually a request for a proof. Just offer the evidence, and let the prospect make the decision on it's validity. More talk proves nothing.

The Waffle as a Way of Life

Some folks get stuck. They won't say yes and don't know how to say no. They waffle:

- "Send us a proposal."
- "Sounds great. Let's do it next year."
- "I'd like to say yes, but how can I sell something like that up top?"
- "I can't approve it, everybody will want it."
- "The timing's not right."
- "I like it, but my boss will say no."
- "Okay, but how will it really work. How do you know, really know?"
- "The needs analysis is not finished."

They're really saying, "No, I don't want it (the product/ service)"; "No, your answer doesn't fit my question"; "No, you didn't make your case."

Salespeople often collaborate with a waffle. We are so afraid of "no" that we decide to believe and act on the waffle. We wait, we watch, we wonder. After a while, frustration rises and we corner the prospect. "You really mean no don't you?" "Why are you saying no?" We take each reply as an objection to be overturned. Each objection is demolished. The prospect is defenseless, yet we all know these people will not buy. Because they can't or simply don't feel like it or are not convinced or ... or ... or. Pushing a prospect into a corner so they must make a public acknowledgement is a loser for everybody and the end of the relationship.

All of us are taught to waffle at an early age. Remember when your mother asked you to clean up your room or do some other odious task. Remember what happened if you flatly said no. Mom would always ask, "Why not?"

You: "I don't have time."

Mom: "Whaddaya mean you don't have time?"

You: "I wanna meet Joe and Charley."

Mom: "You shouldn't even be seeing those two."

And so it went. You quickly learned to say, "Okay, I'll get to it tomorrow" and then deal with the future as it came. In other words – you waffled. A lesson well learned in youth is used throughout life.

Mothers tend to have ways of eventually getting what they want from a waffler, but you have no such power over your prospects. A Waffle is a NO, so act on it. Tell the prospect, "I don't think we're going to do business" – and mean it. State the reasons. You probably know them better than the prospect. If there's a *no* out there and you *know* it, be the first to say so, not the last to hear it. You establish your credentials by being insightful and anticipatory. If you must be led by the hand, why do business with you. You're not bringing anything to the party. Keep the relationship separate from the deal. This chance may be down the drain, but if the relationship remains, there will be another chance. They owe you one.

In life, many love affairs dribble away. The pair drifts apart, often with bitterness and rancor. People seldom say, "Hey, this is over, but there's enough liking left to continue as friends … what do you say?" Business is easier. End a deal cleanly so you can keep connected for other opportunities.

Going Left

Dealing with wafflers or ambiguous global objections – "It won't work here"; "It's too soon" – is tough. You can't really challenge their expertise. They're expert on their business as you are expert on yours. As you try to overcome the objection or explain it away, you just push them in a more negative direction. Your words push them "left."

In the face of real resistance, far better for you to become even more negative. In effect, go to the "left" of the prospect. Get on the prospect's team. "You're correct, it is too soon. Perhaps we should forget this idea completely." The prospect will invariably become more positive – "Well it's not *that* bad!"

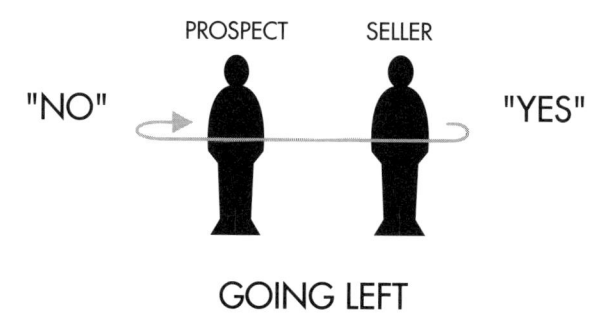

GOING LEFT

This simple role reversal will keep the situation from deteriorating further. Now and then the deal comes back to life when you join the team, but, and it's a big BUT, you're really going left to maintain the relationship, not resuscitate the deal. If you use this as a ploy, the prospect will sense it and both deal *and* relationship will be lost. Unlike my friend Dave, when you "go left" you must be willing to walk.

Dave was a Tazmanian devil! Remember those cartoons where a fuzzy round ball, seemingly all teeth, would chew up everything in its path? That was Dave. I often pictured him turning a skyscraper of potential clients into dusty rubble. Actually, Dave was a pretty good salesman, but greatness would always elude him. He was too hungry and, unfortunately, it showed.

It was a crisp fall day in Philadelphia. Sixty degrees, no wind, a perfect day and probably one of the last before winter. Dave and I were making client service calls: "How's it going?"; "What else can we do?"; "Did you ever consider...?" We were about to have lunch with a client. Dave had put considerable pressure on this account to try one of our new training programs. And Dave, being Tazmanian and all, could really put the heat on.

We awaited the client outside the restaurant. It was just too charged a day to go in any sooner than necessary. Our client arrived and promptly opened the conversation with: "Look, no way I'm gonna buy this program. I've no budget, no time, no interest, no, no, no." We were still on the street. I thought, do I really want to spend my lunch at this fine restaurant on this fine day trying to turn this guy around? The answer was no. My response was: "You know, you're right. It is too soon. Hell, let's forget it. Let's enjoy lunch."

Funny, the more I agreed, the more positive the client became. By coffee, he was even hinting that perhaps a trial run might be possible! In any event, I didn't ask for action. Damn it, I really, truly wanted a relaxed, informal lunch.

As we left, Dave could no longer contain himself. "When can we start? Should I come over next week, tomorrow, later this afternoon to nail down the details?" As you can imagine, our client immediately backed off, much to Dave's confusion and chagrin. Our meeting became a muddle.

Mark McCormack, author of *What They Don't Teach You at Harvard Business School*, writing in *The Wall Street Journal*, makes this point another way: "Backpedal aggressively. There's nothing more refreshing than a salesperson who says: 'This probably is not right for you. Let's defer it for another time.' The best salespeople know that backpedaling in many cases is more important for long-term success than pushing forward full throttle to close a sale. Not only will customers trust you when you say, 'OK, forget this for now,' but they'll be more receptive when you ask, 'Is there anything else we can do for you?'"

Saying Goodbye with Good Grace

A big sale is full of surprises. Most are simply unexpected changes in direction, issue, timing. Some are pleasant. "Can't we start right away?" A few are downright disagreeable. One example: you're meeting, from your view, to confirm the order only to learn that the prospect has given your proposal to a competing salesperson to review.

Here's another: You hit a home run. The economic buyer said, "Let's go for it." In this case, a $275,000 deal. Today the feasibility buyer is on the phone telling you he recommended half the deal and the economic buyer agreed. "Too much too soon," he says. You get the picture. The deed has been done. You're thinking murderous thoughts.

Your response should always be positive, no matter how much it hurts. Remember the action's been taken. The prospect or buyer knows they've brought bad news. They expect a negative reaction. It might have taken courage to call. Before you jump, remember they cared enough to tell you. Some folks would simply let you find out on your own.

Being positive is disarming. Making the best of a bad situation is one of the hallmarks of a star. So your proposal went out the door. "How else can I help?"; "Does she (other salesperson) need other data?"; "It probably makes good sense to have somebody else take a look." Make it O.K. for people to bring you bad news. If you don't burn your bridges, you might come up with a clever strategy to get back on track. It's the stuff you don't know that kills you.

A word about proposals. Now and then somebody will ask for a proposal. Never do a proposal as a speculation. The great majority of projects were done deals at the pre-proposal stage. A speculative proposal is like buying a lottery ticket, and your chances of winning are just as likely. A proposal should only contain what was envisioned or agreed upon during a meeting. It is a confirmation letter, not a sales brochure. Don't fall into the trap of trying to sell with the written word, it can't be done.

The buy is an emotional event. People don't buy on facts, they buy on their *feelings* about the facts. Ultimately, every decision is based on trust. You don't create the mood with a business letter.

Even the best salespeople get told no – a real No Sale no. Professionals believe what they *know*. They don't ask why and risk more irritation. Yes, more irritation. The prospect has spent money on you – time, brain power, hope – and it didn't work out. Stars don't keep pushing. They say, "I wish you well. Perhaps we'll do business in the future if your situation changes." They're supportive. This is a true professional attitude. It leaves the prospect with the nagging feeling that you and your service may be just as good as you say. You're cool, calm, collected, not a prickly, pushy pest. The door is still open for your next call. Remember Saul on the road to Damascus. Never rule out the possibility of a conversion.

Chapter 11 Magic Matters

Is selling a science or an art? The prevailing wisdom shouts "science" at the top of its lungs, but the world is not nearly as simple and straightforward as that.

There is always the question of interpreting the facts (the real truth?). You got a smirk from the bank teller. He calls it a smile. A peer says she's on your side, but you know she isn't. A prospect tells you he can't wait to get started, but you know it's really over. An employee claims to be "taking that extra step" for you, but you know it's not true. A sixth sense tells you what's really happening.

For example, twenty years ago pro quarterbacks personally called all the plays on the field. Then technology was recruited – films, video, computer analysis. The head coach and two assistants became nine coaches. The number of variables and tendencies studied multiplied tenfold. Soon three to four coaches huddled and transmitted the play from the sideline to the quarterback. The quarterback became a mechanic following orders. But there was always one more variable to look at. Soon the analysis process became as complicated as the subject under study. Bit by bit, the essence of the game got lost. Football is still a match between human beings, well-trained magnificent animals, not computer programs.

Increasingly, coaches are turning the game back to the quarterbacks. They are beginning to realize that the key to a game could be, and often is, the intuitive sense that a certain play will work. Or it may be something as simple *and* as incredibly complex as a quarterback "seeing" confusion in the eyes of an opposing cornerback and deciding to run the ball that way.

Slowly, like the pro football coaches, we who sell for a living are coming to the realization that analysis and technique can turn a mechanic into a craftsman, but to win at the professional level, more is required. The players must be artists and leaders – creative, intuitive, flexible, assertive. Sales, football, life are still games of technique *and* touch!!

Believe What You Know

"Touch" begins with the awareness that you know a lot more than you can prove.

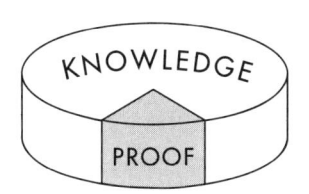

We learn things through the eye of the soul. If you wait for proof to affirm what you believe to be true, it may not be worth knowing anymore ... the sale may be lost.

I remember an incident when I was a kid. I noticed a girl and boy talking quietly in the schoolyard. You could tell they were getting to like each other. I mentioned it to the boy next to me at recess – a smug little kid, a real smart-alecky sixth-grader. I said, "Hey, Jimmy, it looks like there's something going on over there." He turned to me and sneered, "Prove it!" (Remember those kids? Real little snots!)

Prove it? What can you prove about a relationship? People like Jimmy remind me of the little inchworm in the children's song, who steadfastly "measures" the marigolds, but fails to see how beautiful they are. They don't realize that sometimes what matters the most – insight, understanding, intuition – can't be measured.

I ran into a friend in New York City one winter day. He looked terrible! "I just got fired," he told me. I suggested we go somewhere for coffee. Apparently my friend had been abruptly terminated that morning, told to clear his desk and go. (A real humanitarian firm.) He was at loose ends, no prospects, no plan. We talked a bit more and I asked, "When did you first know you were in trouble?" His reply floored me. "Oh, about six months ago." He had begun to sense he was in trouble, but like so many of us, he couldn't take action on what he knew. He had to wait until someone proved it to him. So here he was floundering because he wouldn't act on what he sensed. That would be irrational. It wouldn't be scientific.

Building faith to act on what you *know* rather than what you can prove takes time and some risk on your part. In order to be a sales star, you must be the first to know, not the last to find out. If you see a question mark cross the face of a prospect, *know* that you're in trouble. Act then. Ask about it. You may not get an answer, but you'll demonstrate a lot about your competence as a human being and as a sales professional. Waiting for some overt statement (proof) before acting, will soon have you eating the bark off trees. Soichoro Honda has commented, "I hate college graduates, they only use their heads." You must *unlearn* your ABCs (Always Be Certain).

Tune In

Don't restrict your knowledge or understanding of sales situations to what actually is said. According to many experts on language, spoken words are only a small part of the total communication taking place.

Our forebears first communicated with gestures, grunts and groans and did so for over five-million of our six-million-year existence. Our gestures, body language, inflection, timbre, rhythm, silences, pauses, half smiles, "looks" carry most of the message.

It's the melody that matters. If a mixed message is coming your way, it will sound *and* look off-key. Listen to the melody in your meetings with clients and prospects. Tony Hillerman, in his mystery novel *Coyote Waits*, catches this notion perfectly: "[She] let the sentence trail off intending to let the skepticism in her tone finish it." The melody is like a canary in a coal mine, it provides an early warning.

Non-verbal communication is frequently described in literature. John Le Carré has a character describe his famous agent, George Smiley, "… listening to me long after I finished speaking." Sigmund Freud said of a patient, "If his lips are silent, he chatters with his fingertips."

You should be interested in the *impressions* people give off as much as the words – *expressions* – they say. Your intuitive antenna and receiver are already in place. Just turn the set on! Here are a few ways to test whether or not your intuition, your gut feel, is on the mark:

- You begin to sense, as you're talking to a colleague, prospect or client, that you've lost them on the way. Stop talking, ask: "Am I making this clear or is it getting confused?"
- You're feeling bored with the sales call, but the prospect seems attentive. Stop, ask: "Am I on the point?"
- When you hear that ping on your sonar that tells you something is amiss, stop and check it out.

When all is said and done, the only way to learn if your intuition is tuned in is to take the risk. Your mind is a fine instrument, finer than your awareness of its capabilities. If you sense it's time to leave, leave. If you feel somebody wants to buy something, close. If you feel somebody is upset with you, ask. You must be in front of the wave, not in it, to ride today's economic rapids. The world is not going to wait for the facts to come in before it moves on.

So-so pool players line everything up – the cue ball, the ball in play, the pocket, the cue stick, their line of sight; then promptly miss the shot. They are mechanics and always will be. Experts have a kind of "field vision." They are able to pull back from the action/reaction level. They are mindful, but not analytical. They have a "feel" for the whole table. Star salespeople can pull back from the words being said, turn on the "field vision" and sense what's really going on, the relationships, the mood, the fears. They listen to silence and hear volumes. They see, hear, feel things that others ignore.

Moods Move People

Very few people will acknowledge that they have moods or feel moody now and then. I suppose most people see moodiness as a flaw, an admission of being human, flesh and blood. That, apparently, is something to avoid. Heaven forbid we admit to being human. Still, moods do move people.

Nobody buys an idea, another meeting, or the big deal itself unless they're "in the mood." So much has been said and written about rational decision-making, that one is inclined to believe the nonsense. My experience has been that the cost/benefit rationale is only sought after the choice has been taken. Moods are magical. Clients will never buy unless they're in the mood. They have to feel like they "want to do something."

Moods matter. If a prospect is in a good mood, you're likely to get a positive response. On the other hand, somebody in a bad mood will never buy, no matter how powerful your case. You can be so good they can't say no. They won't say yes either. They'll tell you "the timing's not right."

Carl Jung, the Swiss psychoanalyst wrote, "Emotions are contagious." Recent research affirms his observation and suggests that the interplay of moods between people is very subtle. A recent study by Dr. Ellin Sullins of Northern Arizona University focused on sets of two volunteers facing each other without speaking, ostensibly waiting for instructions. The individuals had been chosen because one was highly expressive of emotions, the other more reserved.

After two minutes, the experimenter asked each volunteer to fill out a mood checklist. It was discovered that the mood of the more expressive volunteers had taken over the mood of the test partners. Apparently this occurred through body language. The effect seems to be instantaneous as well as unconscious.

I happened to be in Minneapolis the day a Blessing/White salesman was making his first call at Sperry-Univac. I was flabbergasted. My guy talked the product to death. It was one incomprehensible product detail after another. I had lived with the product for ten years and I couldn't make head nor tail of the presentation. Pity the poor fellow across the desk. One thing was obvious, however. My salesman believed. The intensity was palpable. There was electricity in the room. Beads of sweat appeared on his brow. The words were a jumble, but the message came through clearly. He had the faith. He was persuasive. He created a mood. The prospect wanted to "get up and go." The prospect wanted to learn more, and he did. Sperry-Univac became our first mega-account.

Your enthusiasm for your product is transmitted by more than words. My guy in Minneapolis hadn't seen the research, but he *knew* that the energy he projected mattered.

Be Positive

I have dozens of cousins, all of whom needed godparents. My aunts and uncles rapidly ran out of other aunts and uncles for this job, so older nephews and nieces were pressed into service. Thus I became the teenage godfather of Glenn, eighth child of Aunt Harriet and Uncle George. As Glenn grew up, nothing was expected of me, and nothing was offered, except the ritual birthday card (my wife remembered).

Several decades, children, jobs, homes later, I heard he was working in New York City, 60 miles away. I had last seen him at his baptism. Here was a chance to see a cousin, my godchild, and learn more about the curious paths my large extended family had taken.

Glenn was a few years out of college, with a good job in a large engineering firm. He arrived at noon on a Saturday and by 2:00 p.m. I was ready to kill him! His job was going nowhere, his meal allowances were too low, but that wasn't too bad because there wasn't any decent place to eat anyway, the weather was or soon would be terrible, there was no use looking for another job, it would be the same old thing, a recession was just around the corner, everything was so boring, what's a fella to do. All of this coming from a bright, good-looking, vigorous young man. He had a terminal case of "poor me."

To shut him up, I put him to work. A support needed replacement under my deck; now seemed the exact moment to do the job. While we were on our backs under the deck, Glenn administered the coup de grace. Some dirt had gotten in one of his eyes and he complained solemnly, "That's the trouble with two good eyes, you're always getting something in them."

Glenn is an extreme case. But how many of us carry at least mild symptoms of self-pity to work? As sales professionals, our job is to turn folks on, not turn them off. *Moods move people.* If you bring dark, heavy clouds into the room, don't expect smiles of eagerness and anticipation. Buyers want to work with a winner and you've just turned this day, and your chances, into a loser. People expect joy when they buy. Positive feelings are part of the purchase.

You must add energy to your encounters with clients. Enthusiasm is truly contagious. Studies have shown that if depressed people force smiles, their depression lifts. Optimistic salespeople sell far more than those with a pessimistic world view. Sales stars are always passionate. They create a mood to act. After all, if you can't get excited about your product, why should others. As Tug McGraw of the Amazing Mets said, "Ya gotta believe."

It's hard to make something happen in this complex, ambiguous world. Prospects know this. Your job is to motivate them to give it one more try. Sales magic starts with your attitude toward life. If you come to the party flat, dull and dreary, don't expect to be invited back.

Make Accidents Happen

The most overrated activity in sales is planning. Much has been claimed for the process and little has been delivered. Obviously, we all need some structure and strategy for our efforts. But with today's events moving at lightning speed, the plan will be out of date before the ink is dry. It's doubtful the future ever did run out in a straight line and, for sure, it doesn't today. Over the years, I found that the best sales plans always came from the weakest salespeople. My best salespeople instinctively knew that a plan was no substitute for action.

When Anthony Eden became Prime Minister of England in the 1950s, hopes were high. He was considered to be the brightest, best-educated, most well-rounded Prime Minister since Disraeli. Unfortunately, his tenure was marked with gaffes, missed opportunities and disasters such as the Suez Canal crisis. Later, when interviewed about this unfortunate turn of events, he was asked, "Did you not have plans?" His response: "Plans, yes we had great plans, but you see, events got in our way."

I spent 17 years working with thousands of people on career management. I learned one absolute principle: Nothing, nothing ever turns out as you plan. I would meet people months, years after they participated in our workshop...

- "Say, did you ever get that promotion you wanted?"

  "Yes."

  "Congratulations. How's it going?"

  "It's terrible, I'm going to quit."

- "Sorry to hear you were laid off."

  "Actually, it worked out just fine. I got a better job in Santa Fe where I always wanted to live."

I was speaking to a buyer of my services at Chase Manhattan. I mentioned my plan to be at his building. Should we get together? No. Anything brewing that I should know about? No. How's it going? Fine. The next day, I was at One Chase Plaza on other business. The elevator in which I was descending stopped at Rich's floor. Why not stick my head in and say hello? I did, and Rich said, "Am I glad to see you. Come in and close the door." As it turned out, he needed to respond to a training problem in the branch system. The issue had been on his desk for weeks! For whatever strange, never to be discovered reason, neither my phone call nor his knowledge of my products had clicked. Sticking my head in his door at 10:30 did. It turned into a $100,000 sale, not peanuts in the training business in 1980!

Most of nature is irregular and apparently random – waterfalls, mountains, coast lines. A new science called chaos is devoted to researching these phenomena. Chaos theorists use an expression – the butterfly effect – that captures how things happen in nature. Apparently it's possible for a butterfly to flap its wings in Beijing and cause a tornado in Kansas. They tell us that in complex environments a small change can create enormous effects.

We certainly are selling in a complex, confusing environment today. Often, serendipity or the random, unplanned action creates momentum. Break a pattern, make the call that's not needed, be unpredictable. Throw a few small unusual actions into your client/prospect world. Turn a few butterflies loose. Make an accident happen!

Believe in Magic

One of my salesmen, a tireless worker, announced that he was turning back an account for reassignment. This came as no small shock to me, since he had never willingly relinquished any prospect. Apparently his contact at Baby Products, a division of Johnson & Johnson, had told him, after a year of discussions, that under no circumstances would they be buying outside services in the foreseeable future. They were adamant. The door was closed with a bang. Since this was as dead as they got, I suppose my salesman felt he could afford to make an altruistic gesture.

A few days passed. I got a call from Baby Products. They were looking for my guy. They wanted to buy now! And they did. I never knew why. Even our buyer was uncertain. This happens more frequently than you would expect. Something happened somewhere. Unpredicted, unplanned, unknown. That damn butterfly again.

A year later, J & J was becoming a large account. My salesman was asked to tell the client's story at our annual meeting for the benefit of our new salespeople. He told a grand story of perseverance (his, of course), planning and strategic thinking. It was terrific material with my guy at the center pulling all the strings. Too bad it wasn't true.

Now, my fella wasn't a megalomaniac, or stupid. His recollection of events was typical. As the 19th-century physicist Ludwig Boltzmann said: "Only half our experience is ever experience." We make up the rest. When we look back, the accident, the chance, long periods of inaction, the retreats, the dozens of calls, all disappear or get truncated as we put our tale together. It makes a good story. It moves in a straight line. It begins and ends. Everything makes sense. No inconvenient facts muddy the water.

People don't want to believe that chance plays such a big role in events, because it makes the world seem so uncertain. The truth is that chance, accident, surprises play a much bigger part in the selling process than we'd like to admit. We make seemingly small decisions and events unfold in ways we could never have predicted from an analysis of the choices we faced.

There's a sign in a Harvard laboratory that reads: "Rats under carefully controlled conditions will do any damn thing they please." People are even worse.

Does this mean that you are always at the mercy of random actions and events? Not if you use some magic to get things going your way. When success depends on your ability to predict and anticipate behavior, your intuition is your best tool and you *must* use it. When you're face-to-face with the client, your energy, enthusiasm and faith in your product will create a willingness to take action.

Finally, just as a map is not the territory, a plan is not action. Put some possibilities out there. Some actions turn out right, some wrong. Unfortunately, consequences are hard to predict in advance. But doing *something*, even if you're unsure of the outcome, is better than inaction. Part of your job is to create incidents, accidents that can, like that butterfly, get something started. Magic matters. Make it happen!

Chapter 12: Tools of the Trade

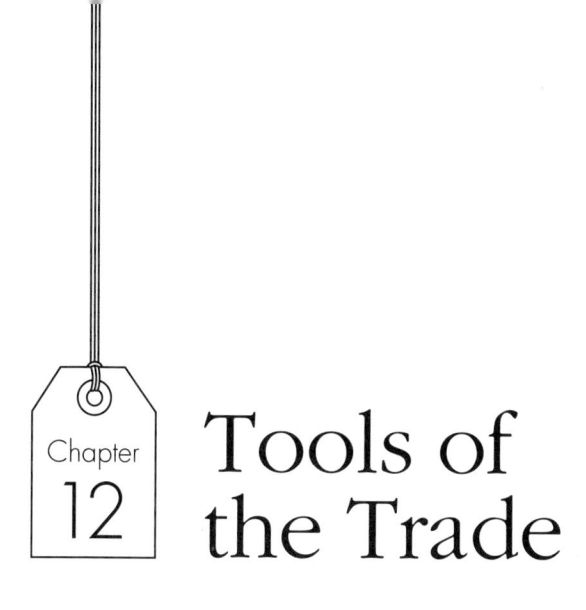

Eliminate fear, uncertainty and doubt in the prospect's mind and the sale is made. Legions of IBM salespeople have heard that admonition. IBM has it right. Ambiguity, insecurity and confusion will kill a deal in a New York minute. But like much advice, its a little short on the how.

Uncertainty is the parent of fear and doubt. For example, prospects might be afraid that a proposed telephone system won't do the job. Are they afraid of the system itself? Obviously not. Their fear stems from uncertainty about whether the system will work as promised.

In general, uncertainty comes into our lives and our customer's world in two ways:

- The natural randomness of the world. The unpredictable events, accidents and serendipities over which we have no control.

- The imprecision and vagueness in the way we speak and communicate. The tongue is the most used, least trained muscle in our bodies.

There's not much we can do to make the world more predictable, but we can and should work on our language. There are at least 600,000 words in the English language and the number increases each day. That's more than enough for clarity, but the average well-read person probably has a vocabulary of 15,000 words and uses 1,500 to 2,000 in a normal week's conversation. That's not much range when you're trying to describe the subtlety of a relationship or the finer differences between you and your competition.

Because of this limited repertoire, some words are vastly overused and have greatly divergent meanings to different people. Several years ago, I called on one of the television networks to discuss their personnel development activities. I talked with the manager of this department for 20 minutes or so and began to sense something amiss. To me, development meant individual career planning. I asked, "What do you mean by 'development' here?" His response: "Development means learning to do what you're told or we fire you!" A bit more specificity earlier would have saved us both time.

The context creates the meaning for what you say. Take the word "overlook." You might say to someone, "You've been overlooked." Depending on the context, their response might be anything from "Thank God" to "That does it!"

Imagine two guys in a locker room. One has just told of an amorous adventure. His buddy responds, "You dog, you!" When his girlfriend hears of this exploit, she exclaims, "You dog, you!" Clearly, the meaning and emotional charge of that expression changed. Few words have exactly the same meaning twice because the context is always shifting.

Some language is simply woo-woo – mushy, pseudo-scientific babble – as in "to crystallize and add velocity to realization of your vision." (An "objective" of an executive development program of a major commercial bank.) Or gobbledygook – incomprehensible jargon – as in "shift from privileging a particular body of culturally sanctioned texts to emphasizing the modes of critical inquiry." (The statement of purpose for a college faculty study committee.)

Obviously, clear language has many enemies:

- Our vocabulary is limited
- We differ on definitions
- The context controls the meaning
- We just don't get it

Tools of the Trade

Words are the tools of your trade. Some tools need regular maintenance, others need occasional sharpening and replacement. More tools are better. Having a special tool for a unique, complicated task will always make life easier. Using a tool properly is the mark of an artisan, a skilled craftsman.

In all sales, and especially in major-account selling, you have two major tasks to accomplish. First, energize the prospect to act and, second, reduce uncertainty. So-so salespeople drift through monotonous monologues of mind-deadening generality. "Well, we … ok … we, uh, we improve the strategic efficiency of …oh … through … you know …" and then wonder why nothing happens.

Getting the words just right and choosing the sequence of words that can clarify an issue, or arouse someone to action, is the core of your profession and your success. Clarity reduces uncertainty. It is your words that move a prospect's heart from "thump, thump, thump" to a breath-catching "hippity hop."

I once asked a colleague what he was selling: "Oh, computer-based training to improve the coaching skills of managers." Fair enough, I suppose, though my interest was waning before the sentence was finished. It was just so predictable and pedestrian. This is the ho-hum stuff we (you, me, clients) hear all day, every day – eminently sensible and exceedingly dull. The whole purpose of speaking is to communicate information not yet known or completely understood. Look, if it's 95% expected, why say it? Who cares? What difference does it make?

My colleague could have responded: "Managers know how to look up the organization. They even know how to look around, but they need to be taught to look down. That's my business, teaching managers how to look down." It's hard to catch the lively tones of the spoken word on the printed page, but I'm sure a prospect would not have shut down the brain cells till that word sequence was finished. In fact, I'd wager that his or her brain cells would have become more agitated. The words were unexpected and novel. This was information coming down!

Our third president, John Quincy Adams, according to historians, was a most unpleasant man. So, there you have some information – an unpleasant president. It didn't move you to the edge of your chair or conjure an image in your mind, did it?

Think about selling. Your job is to get people to sit up and take notice. Our historians surely didn't make that happen, but try these words from a contemporary of Adams: "He had a vinegary aspect, cotton in his leather ears and hatred in his heart." Wow! That's language to stop you in your tracks.

This is the kind of graphic language you need to get to the top of our profession.

Like any artisan, you're always looking for new or better tools and materials. You do it by reading. Read outside your field. Look for words that help you describe what you do more clearly. Find other words for the ones you're currently using. Increase your vocabulary. Expand your ability to say what you mean.

Next, write to speak well. If you plan to make five points in your next presentation, write them out beforehand. If you can't write it, forget trying to say it. You're on the way to woo-woo: "You know, like we're trying to improve productivity with, uh, more sharper focus and getting to people so they get into the vision thing earlier than they would if we didn't get their ownership as soon as we could if it were a top priority." Real snooze material. A blink, a yawn, a snore, the door.

Here's a task you only need to do once in order to create more energy at every sales call: "I'm the economic buyer. I'm feeling pain. I've heard you folks do good work so I phoned. I'm willing to meet, but first I want you to write me a one page letter telling me why it makes sense to get together. I want to get moving on this. Could I have it in a couple of days?" Believe me, your sales presentations will never be the same after you write this memo. It will force you to answer in a succinct way – "Hey, why should I give you money." Surely, that is a question that deserves, no requires, a crisp answer.

Understanding is insured only if you can make a point or clarify a situation in a variety of ways. Actively seek metaphors, similes, analogies, alliterations and examples in your presentations to clients. Using these figures of speech at *every* opportunity triggers energy. They get an emotional response and intensify the orientation to action.

Your artistry in sales is in your words, but the length of time you talk or the number of syllables will not be the measure of your success. True art in words is plain, colorful, accurate language. It is your ability to use surprising combinations of words and to communicate fresh, unexpected information.

Getting the Steam Up

Descriptive language crafted into compelling stories is basic to success in selling. No stories, no sales!

Stories are real! They describe situations similar to the prospect's. Prospects compare the stories you tell with their own experiences. This is the only way to really see your "stuff" at work.

Stories build the relationship! You "show up" as you relate clear, sharp anecdotes. If they're on point, the prospect will see you are credible and insightful. But even if they don't quite hit the mark, they will elicit comments and questions. As stories bring questions, your answers bring respect.

Stories create energy! Good stories get people's interest and attention. You'll see it. They sit up, sometimes wake up, when someone starts to tell a story. Juices start to flow. Nobody can sell in a lifeless room. People need a dose of energy to get moving. Listen to Nanno Marinatos describing her father, the late Greek archaeologist, Spyridon Marinatos:

> *He was a great story teller. He described to me how he imagined things were, how people lived... The stories my father told me – they weren't stories in the*

sense of a narrative about people walking through dead corridors; they were told more in the tone of a search. They were questions put together in such a way as to make the problem exciting. You wanted to dig the next day and see – was he right, or must we revise the theory?

This man knew how to energize his listeners. Would that we all could do as well.

Stories sell! They let you show that an "issue" can turn into "trouble" for the prospect. Remember, people pay money to get rid of trouble; getting rid of an issue is less important – "maybe next year" is always soon enough. Trouble, on the other hand, means that bad things are going to happen if the prospect fails to act.

You Got Trouble . . . . . Right Here in River City

Harold Hill, "The Music Man," had it right. A school band would be a nice thing for River City, but he knew the town fathers would never spend big money for that opportunity. He had to create dissatisfaction with current affairs.

Professor Hill was not a Ph.D. However, Dr. Amos Tversky of Stanford University is, and he says much the same thing. According to a report in the *New York Times*, Dr. Tversky describes a "mental accounting" by which people evaluate potential gains and losses. People are more sensitive to negative consequences than positive outcomes. He believes this concern is genetic. Apparently, our prehistoric ancestors who worried less may have been happier, but those saber-toothed tigers got a lot more of them than the worrywarts. Ergo, we'll spend money quicker to fix trouble than to capture an opportunity.

Here's a graph Professor Hill and Dr. Tversky could agree with:

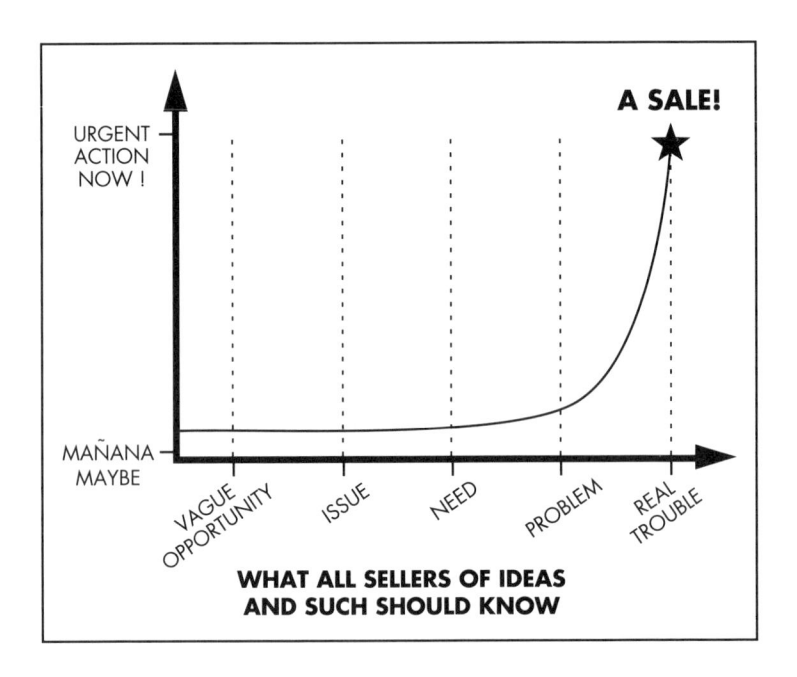

```
                                              A SALE! ★
   URGENT
   ACTION
   NOW !




   MAÑANA
   MAYBE
           VAGUE      ISSUE   NEED   PROBLEM   REAL
           OPPORTUNITY                         TROUBLE

              WHAT ALL SELLERS OF IDEAS
                  AND SUCH SHOULD KNOW
```

Very rarely does trouble, real trouble, march into your prospect's office. If it does, it usually takes the form of the boss saying, "Fix this or else." Most personal agendas are filled with ought-to-do's, annoyances and ambiguous needs. Oh, there's trouble around, but for some reason people don't see it, like Wile E. Coyote in the "Road Runner" cartoons, until it's too late. Disaster cannot be avoided.

Several years ago, I was working with a newly appointed Director of Training at Kimberly-Clark. He had been given a mandate by the Chairman to install a new organization development system. Two years later, he was still reviewing options, doing research, and interviewing consultants (myself included). He was the classic analytic type. All this guy needed was a pipe, an overstuffed chair and a springer spaniel to make him complete. Over lunch, I suggested that he take action soon or he would be gone. That recommendation was dismissed out of hand. He was sure his Chairman wanted it done "right." That Training Director never got his chance to do it right. He was fired within the month. He just didn't know he was in trouble. Unfortunately, I wasn't able to "sell" the fact that he was.

More often than not, your job as a seller is to help potential clients understand the nature of the situation they face. They know there's a problem, they just don't know it well enough! Unless they see they've got "trouble, real trouble, right here in River City," action is unlikely to occur. People who feel no pain don't buy. Your job is to make them aware of their dissatisfaction with the current state of affairs. "Things can be better, much better"; "Things will get worse, much worse!" The more dissatisfaction, the greater the eagerness to find a solution. *People pay money to get rid of trouble.*

Warnings don't work. Goat shows seem nice, but who really cares? What does help is stories – word pictures. Pictures with people in them. Pictures of problems that can be "seen" by the buyer. Often the points we should make most powerfully are stated in the weakest way. Here's an example: "The objective is to improve communications." This is clinical, unemotional language. No juices get stirred up. Here it is as a metaphor: "Our service will get rid of the 'I don't know, not my job' disease your clerical staff has caught."

That's a statement you can feel. The potential buyer knows exactly what is supposed to get better and will be delighted when it happens. The first example gave a result. The latter was the beginning of a story. It had impact.

I've had the good fortune to work with several terrific salespeople. Passionate, emotional, human, energetic and energizing storytellers every one. They had something that made a difference: They were eager to tell their story and it was always a real story – exciting, dramatic, filled with detail, metaphor and analogy. One always asked, "Would you like to learn more?" A yes would invariably elicit another story. Another sales star *only* told stories! Stories bring energy into the room. No big ticket sale is made without them.

The Elements of a Good Story

Here's a fax machine salesman in the mid-eighties, talking about his new product:

> *The world is changing. There's a real shortage of trained clerical workers. We had a baby boom – 65 million people – but they're growing older and moving on. Now we have a baby bust of only 28 million people in the 18-30-year range. The labor pool is tight.*
>
> *Nobody can find help. Just look at all the "Help Wanted" signs in store windows. The other day I went into a 7-11 store to get a sandwich. On the board showing that day's Special were the words "BAKIN LETTIS." It took me a while to figure out that the Special was a bacon, lettuce and tomato sandwich. I guess they just gave up on "tomato."*

> *Some of the best workers aren't in the work force anymore, maybe raising children, maybe looking for part-time self-employment. Who knows? A couple of years ago there was no way to connect with these people quickly. If you wanted to use them for clerical support, it was either dictation over the phone or the U.S. mail. Lots of chance for something to go wrong or go slow. The fax machine has changed all that. For a few hundred bucks, a small business can get top quality clerical help operating from home and the efficiency of an in-house employee. The fax is a tool of the future.*

I love this guy. He's got stories to tell. He's thought about the world. He believes in his stuff. People wanted to hear more. Soon he was talking more issues, then how his company or product was different from others. He sold a lot of fax machines.

What made that story good? Stories that work always include people. You can see their behavior. You can easily imagine the consequences of their actions. Clients don't buy just because they have a problem. They buy because of the effect of the problem on people; the noise others are making about equipment, systems and procedures that don't work or the poor performance of the people doing the work. That's why your stories must have people in them.

The *BAKIN LETTIS* anecdote was great. It was novel. It was unexpected. It made the point about the lack of qualified workers more powerfully than any amount of statistical data. It truly was information! It was short and to the point, not a shaggy dog. Always tell a story so that the beginning is not forgotten before the end is reached.

The language was colorful and colloquial. It was all facts, issues, problems. No polysyllabic fog here. Some people believe using big words establishes their credibility. That may work in some situations, but between seller and buyer plain talk is always more powerful.

Finally, our fax salesman answered a very important question for the potential buyer in the last few sentences of his story, i.e., "What will be better as a result of doing business with you?"

Stories – Two Sources

Talk to clients. How are they using the product? The first answer you get will be the objective: to increase productivity, to improve distribution, to develop a Total Quality culture and so on and so on. Vague glutinous statements full of woo-woo and gobbledygook. These are not stories! This is the kind of verbiage our competition talks. We can do better.

The best stories are about people doing something differently as a result of your product or service: "Our engineers spent all kinds of time moaning and groaning about our slow computers, how user-unfriendly they were. Now we don't hear a word."

Now you've got the beginnings of a story. You need more detail. My guess, though, is the person in front of you at this moment doesn't know one more thing. You're probably talking to the feasibility buyer. He's not the person with the problem. That's the economic buyer – the person who said, "The problem reports to me." That's the person with the adjectives, the expletives, the details. That's the restless sleeper who had an upset stomach over the damn thing.

Talk to her. She'll tell you a story! One that lots of your other prospects have lost sleep over. You'll have to dig for facts, the color that makes your anecdote come alive. Start with economic buyers, follow up with the users of your service. How is their life better? Can they give you an example? Can they tell you a story? And they *will* tell you a story. Most people are eager to tell their story to a willing listener.

Stories are always first person reports. No third person, whether it's a colleague, a manager or a non-economic approver, can give you a story. Their versions have lost sharpness. Facts with glittering, metallic edges turn into dull, vague reports.

Another source of stories is the world around you.

- What's going on? What's happening?
- Why is Hollywood making the movies they do?
- What's on the news?
- What do your neighbors complain about?
- What's on the minds of your professional peers?
- Is there anything in the TV show you just watched that connects to your work?
- What's bothering you? Remember, you're not alone.

Take the time to write out one of your own stories. See if you can make sense of what you are trying to say. Make sure it has real, everyday people in it. You should be able to visualize their behavior. Your story should detail some action in colorful, colloquial language and make your point in a novel, unexpected way.

An accomplished salesperson is always looking for new stories. Is there an example, a metaphor, an analogy that I can pull from this experience that will help me sell? We, like comedians, need fresh material to keep our audience attentive. Just like the humorists, when we're going stale, the whole world knows it.

Diplomats have a saying about treaties: "The devil is in the details." That may be true for them, but in the selling process, the details are pay dirt. It's the descriptive details that arouse the prospect, create the mood and the energy for action. Stories turn prospects into champions and buyers into believers.

Chapter 13: After the Sale

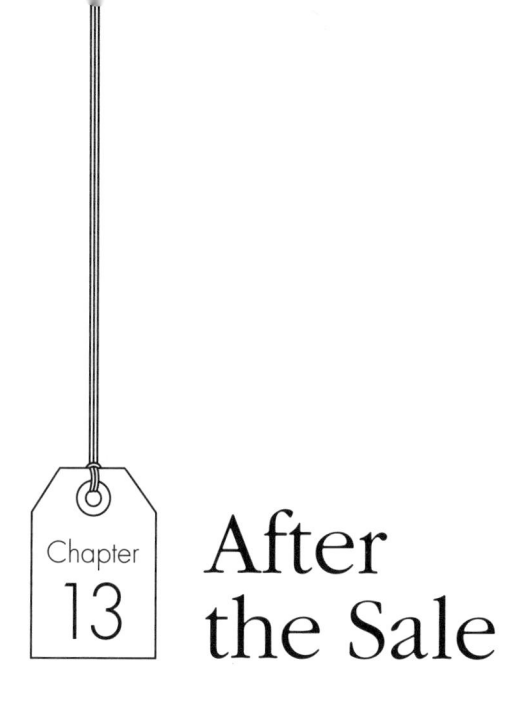

You've made a sale, but like all modern selling, this is just the beginning. It's the first step to the BIG DEAL, the one that makes your year. You're pleased with yourself. Not many could have made this happen. Who would have believed it? All this from a blind date!

After the deal is done, it's easy to forget your partner – the buyer. You may have promised the moon. You owe the buyer. He or she has expectations for service, delivery, follow-up. And don't think that's not your job, either. Your vows are your responsibility, not manufacturing's, or distribution's or anybody else's. It's up to you to see that your company comes through.

Like a marriage partner, you signed on for the long haul. If you make the relationship work, this sale will simply be the first of many pleasant experiences. Only the amateurs among us forget they made a commitment. Professionals want a sale to be the beginning of business, not the end of it.

Now is the time to keep your promises. You always had two clients – the personal needs of the buyer and the goals of the organization. The degree to which you satisfy both is directly related to repeat business. What is your buyer gaining from this transaction? How are you going to insure that result? Don't expect buyers to forget what they wanted from the deal. They never forget, ever.

If you've got a good relationship, the buyer will probably trust you enough to tell you what he personally expects to gain. But what if the buyer's needs have not been made explicit? Some would argue you can't know all the personal reasons people buy. That may be true, but knowing is not necessarily the issue. It's caring enough to try to find out in the first place. That's the real difference between the stars and the stand-ins.

Buyer's Remorse

Energy, enthusiasm, confidence and hope were in the room when the sale was made. You're gone now and some of the joy left with you. The buyer is worried, even a bit depressed, wondering if this really was the right thing to do. Think about your last big purchase. Did you walk away without the slightest anxious twinge? Without a little nagging fear that maybe you shouldn't have done it?

Buyers need reassurance. A most formidable saleswoman in a Fifth Avenue clothing store had this lesson down pat. She caught up with every purchaser, after the cash register and before the front door, to say: "The more I picture you in that outfit ... I know it's just right for you." That's a professional. She was so successful she wound up owning the shop.

Many a deal has fallen apart after the sale. Pleasure is in travelling from discomfort to comfort. Pleasure is only at the purchase. Once "it" is bought, it brings obligations, work, risk, maintenance, visibility. "I'll handle the details" was one of the most important promises you made. Remember, you sold "making it easy." To safeguard the sale, always reassure your buyer with a call or letter, reaffirming those promises and the bright, certain success of your buyer's purchase.

Set Me Free

Your first sale to this client was just that – a first sale. Your implementation was smooth. The buyer is looking good. Now for bigger game. Unfortunately this buyer can't buy more and has let you know how unhappy she would be if you went hunting.

Those feelings are understandable. Every day money is pouring into her psychological bank account from doing business with you. The program, product, service is doing the job in a highly visible way. That's good. She's got your undivided attention. That's even better. She has an exclusive on you and your staff. That's the best! Ah, to be the first and only one in your gang with a genuine Duncan yo-yo. It's hard to forget.

To ignore the buyer's feelings now turns a friend into an enemy. To avoid this problem, you need to ask permission *after the sale and before implementation* – "Now assuming this works, as we expect, I would want to contact … (peers, managers, senior executives). I'll need your help." Or asking,

"What's our plan for success?" is another good way to gain agreement for you to spread your wings. Make it part of the tacit agreement – the unwritten "what's in it for you, what's in it for me." She may accept a quid pro quo at the time of the sale. Once the reviews are in and your buyer becomes a star in a hit, she will be most unwilling to move off center stage.

A Hammer is a Hammer

Reality is in the eye of the beholder. Your buyer has an image of what your product does and over time it's locked in.

For 17 years, Blessing/White sold a training seminar used for individual career development. Ninety percent of our business dealt with that issue. Over 60 major U.S. banks were using the program for career development. Ad campaigns, articles regarding our work were flooding the market. People were attending our career seminar over any other by a margin of 20, 30 to 1.

One bank client in Chicago, however, was using the program for a special, non-career problem in the branch banking system. My buyer had become a personal friend over the eight years we worked together. One winter day, I walked into his office – a meeting without objectives – and asked a "What's up, Doc?" question. His response flattened me! He lamented how much trouble he was having finding a career development program for his people. He proceeded to describe his requirements. They were identical to my program specs. He wasn't kidding, either! He simply never saw my program as more than a special tool for one particular issue.

A hammer is a hammer! Never assume current clients see other possibilities for your product or service. They don't. You must do follow-up marketing. Meetings without objectives are good for this. Sharp, crisp stories of different client applications will interest and inform your clients.

Complaints

The key to maintaining a relationship is complaints. When a marriage is truly dead, there are no more complaints. Stay in touch. Actively seek complaints. Quick resolution of a complaint strengthens a relationship, establishes your effectiveness, shows you care and leads to repurchase 95% of the time. Clients would rather switch than fight. Most people do not bother to complain. They buy something else and tell their friends bad things about their experience with your company.

You can tell whether an organization is a monopoly by the way it handles complaints. Right now, cable TV companies are protected from competition and it shows. I was appointed by my town to be its representative to our local cable supplier. I had a few questions, but answers were hard to get. Finally, I found myself talking to a fellow named John at the cable TV corporate office hundreds of miles away. I got some useful information. I asked John for his last name in case I needed further data. His reply: "Oh, we don't give out last names here." With an attitude like that, cable companies better pray every night for continued legislative protection. If you're not in the cable business, you better be asking for comments and complaints.

After the Honeymoon

When two people enter a relationship, both parties hope for domestic bliss. But people change, interest wanes, attention lags, irritations surface, incompatibilities grow larger. Unless you work at it, the relationship flattens, sometimes dies, more likely becomes comatose. The same is true in sales relationships. Keeping a client requires constant reselling efforts while things are going well, lest the partnership dies when things go wrong. As a client relationship ages, the original benefits, the excitement, the rationale for doing business fade away. A client loss is like a divorce. It's unlikely you even remain friends.

Your relationship with your buyer is your most precious asset. One study shows that 75% of customers who claim to be "very satisfied" will buy a second time, while only 20% of "satisfied" customers repeat. And all customers who are very satisfied also say they have an "excellent" relationship with their salesperson. Never forget that it is your responsibility to keep the fires of client satisfaction burning brightly.

Top professionals schedule regular contact with their clients. They know it takes five times more effort to get a new client than to sell the same amount to a current account.

Chapter 14
The World as a Work of Art

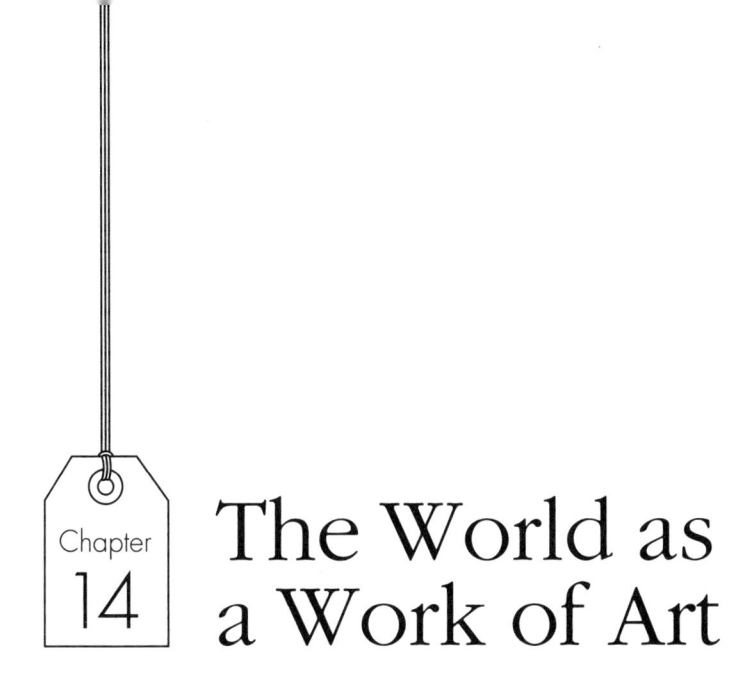

One of the best salespeople I have worked with, when talking about her profession, would say "I'm a philosopher" or "I sell philosophy." She did not see herself as simply pushing a product or service.

She knew that her greatest challenge was to help the client more deeply understand how his or her world worked. Once a client clearly saw the context in which he or she was operating, the salesperson's product or service made a lot more sense and became a lot more important.

What my saleswoman was really saying was that she was trying to broaden her horizon and understand people's motivations more clearly, so she could come up with a big idea, a vision of an exciting and powerful use of her product. She understood a fundamental point about selling. You must know how your stuff makes sense in a bigger way than simply improving quality or increasing productivity. Forget all the tough talk you hear, a client only makes an extraordinary commitment of dollars and time to a vision – some compelling story of his or her world made better by purchasing your product. The bottom line data are for the record; the vision creates the commitment.

It's your job to help the customer see the forest instead of just the trees. But you can't talk the big picture unless you have one. The more you understand the world you live in, the more effective you will be. You must be filled with curiosity. Customers want answers – and the bigger the deal, the bigger the answer must be. To provide that answer, you must be willing to question conventional assumptions about how the world works.

The Big Picture

Everything we see is colored by our understanding of how the world works. We look up at the sky and see a straight trail of water vapor. Our mind's eye might even see a jet plane where none exists. Why? Because our scientific structure of belief tells us that long, narrow "clouds" are caused by jet exhaust. A "pre-scientific" person might interpret the plume as a sign of a visitor from the heavens.

As you read the words on this page, you see a b c's. A Papuan aborigine might see only black marks and, by observing your intense interest in them, conclude that the marks are magical. Medieval people saw devils and angels. Their way of looking at the world let them see spirits – and they did.

The Arab astronomer Ptolemy, believed the sun and stars revolved around the earth. He devised an increasingly elaborate system to explain the planetary motions he observed. His system became hugely complicated, wheels within wheels. It worked, but not very well. A millennium later, another astronomer, Copernicus, suggested that if we reversed Ptolemy's key assumption – if, in fact, the earth goes around the sun – planetary motion could be explained very simply. It was a change in view that changed the world.

A more accurate view of how the world works can make every salesperson more effective and more in control of the selling process. A realistic paradigm helps us put into perspective the events around us, prepares us for what we are likely to encounter, and suggests better, more strategic selling ideas. Clearly, if you have an unrealistic view of how your prospects' relationships, motives, actions develop, you will be ineffective in selling them your product.

The World as a Watch

In 1666, an apple dropped to the ground. That apple determined the way you and I view the world around us, how we judge other people. Even what we believe is important to measure, what is true and what is false.

What an apple! It had such a great effect because Isaac Newton saw it drop. That apple gave us Newtonian mechanics. This new and powerful view of how the world worked took people by storm. Before Newton, we believed in magic. After Newton we believed in science. The world was a machine! There was an order to things! We simply needed to figure out how everything worked.

When science first came on the scene, it applied its methods to simple systems – gases, planetary movement, steam engines; one-, two- or three-variable inorganic problems. Out of that work came the technology we have today, along with beliefs about how the world worked. According to the Newtonian mechanical model of the universe, our world is:

- Linear: A → B → C
- Static, predictable
- A machine, a kind of large watch
- Made up of "parts"
- Quantifiable, measurable
- Gradually changing over time
- Real – there is an objective truth out there
- A place in which 2 + 2 = 4, **always**

Not much to disagree with, right? You get run over by a truck, that's REAL. Four quarters make a dollar, every time. That "lazy ole sun" comes up in the morning. That nail caused my tire to go flat. My television's made of parts and it works. Newtonian science explains much and makes at least part of our world quite predictable. People tried to apply these principles everywhere. Mostly they "worked,"

that is, you could make a prediction and it came true. It was just common sense.

Nevertheless, problems arose, especially when you tried to apply these beliefs to *people*. True to the Newtonian mechanical model, we tried to find out what made people *tick*. But things just didn't work out. Utopian communities based on scientific principles were founded, and vanished in a few years. Stimulus-response theories were applied to elicit behavior. It seemed to work with electric shocks, but a bit of praise from the boss (positive stimulus) could get varied reactions: "Great!" "What's she up to now?" "Cut it out!"

Homo sapiens might believe in logic, but events didn't seem to turn out as expected. Alice and Jeff seemed to be the perfect couple, a marriage made in heaven. It lasted six months. Countless millions of dollars have been spent on performance appraisal systems, yet none of them seems to work. For some reason, they don't measure what matters. "Oh well," people would say, "we didn't have enough facts."

Eventually, scientists began to realize that Newtonian mechanical principles, with their emphasis on cause and effect, had their limitations. While they apply to the workings of an F-15 fighter plane which, for all its sophistication, is made of simple systems, they cannot explain more complex, multi-variable systems like waterfalls, the weather or those laboratory rats at Harvard.

Complex systems work in counter-intuitive ways. Physicists probing atoms discovered that a force could be in two places at the same time. Others studying light rays, discovered that whichever form of light – wave or particle – they decided to observe, that was the form that showed up. In a way, you created what you were looking for! There apparently is no ultimate reality detached from our observations. What we look for is what we see! In many ways, the world we live in, or think we live in, is mostly a world of our own making.

Mathematician Kurt Godel proved that complex systems of logic were not only incapable of demonstrating all the true facts of the system, but were quite capable of producing falsehoods with their own internal logic, so 2 + 2 = 4 wasn't always true!

Gone Fishing

Complex systems never seem to work as predicted. Take trout, for instance. Iridescent, pink-flanked, elegant, a prize fish for any angler. Fly-fishing for trout is almost a religion, at least a ritual – barbless hooks, waxed lines, special flies (hand-tied only, thank you). Fishing in a famous trout stream is like a trip to Lourdes. The solemn, prayerful, hoping-for-a-miracle pageantry is the same.

For more than 50 years, billions of hatchery-raised trout have been dumped in America's precious streams. This was common sense at work. Catch a fish, then replace it, once or maybe even twice, from a hatchery. Yet, contrary to expectations, trout populations continue to fall, and in some lakes and rivers no trout at all can be found. Were they over-fished? No, because fishing and netting were limited as the trout populations diminished. As far as trout were concerned, 2 + 2 could be 3 or even zero.

It seems that hatchery trout, when released, rush around picking fights with the locals. Fish die as a result. Wild trout guard their food supply because they know it is scarce. They can only expend as much energy protecting it as can be replenished. Hatchery trout disrupt this pattern and more wild trout die.

Hatchery trout don't fear humans, who have been feeding them "fish chow" from the beginning. They rush to be caught or become easy pickings for some predator. More trout disappear. Hatchery trout spot wild food less successfully. They get weaker and eventually die out.

Thirty-five years ago any damn fool knew that stocking trout made sense. Now we learn it is a disastrous practice. Life is a lot like that trout stream. It's hard to predict with certainty the results of your actions.

Many of us just don't want to accept that the world is not amenable to simple solutions. We yearn for easy answers to messy questions. Pity the poor trout. Somebody knew just what they needed and gave it to them.

Accu-Weather

So much for trout conservation. Let's take a look at another area where we turn to science for answers – the weather. Now predicting the weather is easy. Predicting it correctly is much more complicated. The European Weather Forecasting Center at Reading U.K. has a CRAY X-MP super computer. The speed of this electronic marvel is measured in megaflops – a megaflop being one million arithmetical calculations per second. The Cray operates at 800 megaflops! Imagine the data being processed in thirty minutes! Yet at best that half-hour of computing time will only provide a so-so prediction of tomorrow's weather in Europe.

I was in London on October 15, 1987, when a hurricane hit Hyde Park with unbelievable fury. Ancient, historic elms, oaks, were blown to the ground. Nearby Kew Gardens, the world-famous arboretum, was almost destroyed. This was the worst storm in Britain since 1703. The weather forecast for that day was light showers, bright intervals and moderate winds. When queries were made, the official response was: "We can predict the weather accurately provided it doesn't do anything unexpected."

Humans are every bit as complex as a trout stream or the weather, yet we persist in looking for superficial explanations of behavior. If a guy jumped from a bridge into that stream, Newtonian science could easily predict how long it would take him to hit the water, but can offer no insight into why he chose to jump in the first place. Which is the more important question?

The Quantum Leap

"Every day in every way I'm getting better and better!" Lots of people believe this *should* be the case, although their personal situation may seem to be a temporary exception. Buried in that statement is a dead-wrong assumption about how people change that belongs to the simple system paradigm. The assumption is that the rate of change is gradual and constant. It can be fast or slow, but it always moves in a straight line.

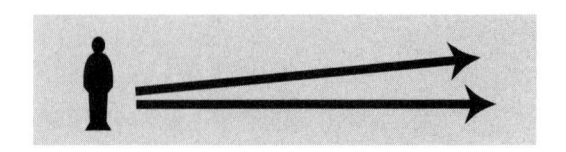

A COMMON BELIEF ABOUT CHANGE

Any statement we make about how people change is of critical importance, because it determines the expectations we have of ourselves, of others, of the world around us. Any assumption we make about how the world works drives our behavior. If we assume the sales cycle to be a gradual, linear process, we will do a lot of planning. The sale will be seen as a routine event that occurs as a result of a salesperson following specific procedures. When you expect the future to roll out of the past in a straight line, method and process get priority. Follow instructions and success will follow.

Much as we might devoutly wish selling to be that easy, no sales veteran has made a major sale according to plan. Accidents, a whimsical mood, a chance encounter, an unbelievable resuscitation of a previously dead prospect have almost always been decisive factors in the drama. Looking at the world through our "scientific" lens, we dismiss these as "strange coincidences" and see only the gradual unfolding of our strategy. But what if our belief about the rate of change is wrong? Could the "coincidences" be more important than we think? Could a major sale in fact develop in a totally different way?

Every day in every way we are not getting better, because that's not the way change comes about in people and organizations. Change rates in complex systems can best be described as long plateaus of no change punctuated by rapid changes to new levels. Change is not gradual, it is *punctuational*. Change is much better described as an uneven set of exercise steps.

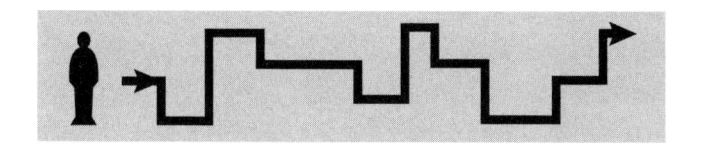

THE ACTUAL WAY PEOPLE CHANGE

Do complex systems really work by periodic, episodic, unpredictable changes? Stephen Jay Gould, the Harvard paleontologist, believes that evolution itself is punctuational: "We are here because events *happened to take particular random turns*, not as a result of a tendency for nature to lead, step by sequential step, up a straight and narrow ladder from intertidal slime to man and civilization." [Emphasis added.]

But the most compelling argument for punctuational change can be found, not in the laboratory, but within yourself and your own personal experiences. What incidents contributed most to your career? Did they come about gradually within your current work responsibilities or were they triggered by some occurrence? Were any of them "accidents"? Have you ever experienced learning plateaus?

Think about building a skill. You practice and practice without much improvement. Then one day – bang! – you're operating on a new level. Remember how you learned to ride a bicycle? A salesperson needs to be opportunistic and sensitive to these hops, skips and jumps. Think about a recent sale. Did it roll right out or did it occur in fits and starts? Did you "guess" right about some action to take?

Every change is triggered by a strong impetus for action. Understanding this concept of punctuational change is central to achieving sales success. A sale requires change in the status quo. You must create energy in the form of stimulating, intriguing, compelling ideas and dramatic actions to overcome the natural inertia of people and organizations. Your most important task as a salesperson is to provide the enthusiasm that gets the process moving.

The World as a Work of Art

Unlike the Newtonian/mechanical model, a complex system is:

- Made of patterns or loops
- Changing punctuationally: the quantum leap
- A work of art, unique, one of a kind
- Made of relationships, invisible connections
- Not "real" – The observer makes it up
- Dynamic, ever-changing
- Qualitative – What matters often can't be measured
- A place in which 2 + 2 = 4, **maybe**

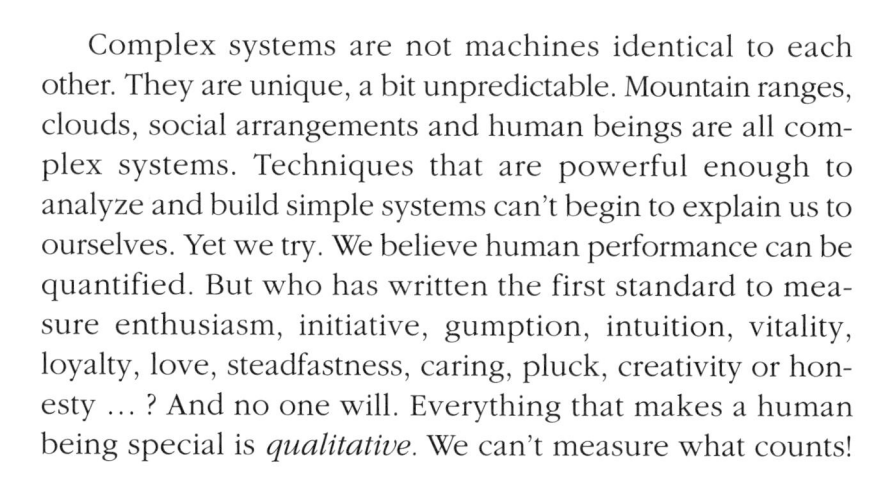

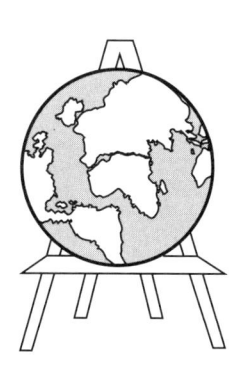

Complex systems are not machines identical to each other. They are unique, a bit unpredictable. Mountain ranges, clouds, social arrangements and human beings are all complex systems. Techniques that are powerful enough to analyze and build simple systems can't begin to explain us to ourselves. Yet we try. We believe human performance can be quantified. But who has written the first standard to measure enthusiasm, initiative, gumption, intuition, vitality, loyalty, love, steadfastness, caring, pluck, creativity or honesty … ? And no one will. Everything that makes a human being special is *qualitative*. We can't measure what counts!

So we measure what we can, which are mostly things that don't matter.

Performance appraisal systems are great examples of how we try to force reality into our belief structure. Hardly any of them work, and employees complain. Managers create elaborate fictions to justify ratings. Goals set in the beginning of the year disappear from priority lists. Unexpected issues and opportunities never find their way into the system. Ratings appear arbitrary. Few can be defended even on a rational level. Yet no one will say it's a failure of theory. It's always a failure of execution: "The form's not right." "Inadequate training." "Lack of top management support." Saying, "This stuff just doesn't work" is frightening. It forces us to rethink our "lens," the structure of belief that helps us make sense of the world. We hate uncertainty, so we just keep trying to make the world fit our assumptions. Just like Ptolemy.

Most sales training is like that, too. The old Newtonian model is simple, predictable, repeatable and measurable. Mediocrity, impersonal competence is good enough in that world. So what if we can't measure intangible qualities like drive or passion? Who needs them in a linear, logical, cost-benefit, rational world? Everything is numbers anyway.

Many sales gurus would have us believe that selling is an analytic, rational process. Alas, the world I live in doesn't seem to have gotten the message yet. Where they see order, I see chaos. Where they see good-looking MBAs around conference tables reviewing long-range plans, I see guys on their knees rolling dice. Where they see cool, clear, rational discussions, I see impulsive, emotional choices being made.

In their world, prospects are seen as machines. A certain stimulus will get a predictable response. In my world, people are impossible to peg. There is as much serendipity as science in making a sale.

The world is not a watch and man is not a machine. Randomness, contrariness, emotions, brilliance, intuition, mystery, risk and changing relationships define the world real people inhabit.

Accepting this reality is the first step on the road to success in sales – and in life. You become a different person as you recognize that moods, chance, magic all play a part in that human interaction we call a sale. The essential step to getting a "vision" of what you and your product or service can do is to have a vision about how this old world works. Selling will be fun, not mechanical. You can be passionate, human, energetic and energizing. Not a bad way to start every day!

About the Author

The author is president of Buck Blessing Associates, a sales training and consulting firm. Prior to forming BBA, he was co-founder and president of Blessing/White, Inc., the largest career management training firm in the world. He has written and lectured extensively on career management, motivation, and major account sales. His ideas have been featured in the *Wall Street Journal, Data Training, Megatrends, Cosmopolitan, Working Woman* and *Entrepreneur.*